I Quit the Family

WHAT MOMS MAY THINK BUT NEVER SAY

Andrea Holman

Andrea Holman

Copyright © 2021 Holman Entertainment, LLC.

All Rights Reserved. No part of this publication may be reproduced, distributed, or transmitted in any form or by any means, including photocopying, recording, or other electronic or mechanical methods, without the prior written permission of the publisher, except in the case of brief quotations embodied in critical reviews, and certain other non-commercial uses permitted by copyright law. For information, please contact info@andreaholman.com.

Scripture taken from the New King James Version®. Copyright © 1982 by Thomas Nelson. Used by permission. All rights reserved.

First edition: 2021

10 9 8 7 6 5 4 3 2 1

Printed in the United States of America.

ISBN: 978-1-7371610-0-4 (trade paper)
ISBN: 978-1-7371610-1-1 (ebook)

Book and cover design by Trent Design
Photography by Tara Lynn Holman

Dedication

I want to dedicate this book to my husband, my kids, and my parents.

To my husband Luke: When we met, God blessed me beyond measure. Without you running, walking, and crawling with me through our unpredictable story, I wouldn't have survived the words that filled the pages. Thank you for your friendship, laughter, love, and support along the way.

To each of my kids, who added their own plot twists and countless sleepless nights: Thank you for the lessons you've taught me. Being your mom is more adventurous and illuminating than I ever expected! You have enriched my life with joy and love!

To my mom and dad: Thank you for showing me how to open my heart to God. It was the most important lesson you taught me and one I have passed to your grandchildren. That legacy of love continues to cover our stories. Thank you for accepting my crazy antics and encouraging me to always be who God created me to be, even when it drove you crazy!

Andrea Holman

"Oh, that You would bless me indeed, and enlarge my territory, that Your hand would be with me, and that You would keep *me* from evil, that I may not cause pain!"

(I Chronicles 4:10)

Contents

Introduction 1

Chapter 1: It's Exhausting Being in Control 7

Chapter 2: 40 Weeks of Pregnancy? 23

Chapter 3: Delivery of a Baby Does Not a Mother Make 51

Chapter 4: I Quit the Family! 79

Chapter 5: Words You're Not Prepared to Hear 109

Chapter 6: No! You Can't Touch Me! 131

Chapter 7: I'm Reaching 157

Chapter 8: Hallelujah! I Can See the Other Side! 175

Conclusion:
The Most Important Lesson I Can Share with You 197

Acknowledgments 199

About the Author 201

Andrea Holman's "I Quit The Family" is a raw, real, authentic story about Motherhood and life that you will enjoy. Andrea's engaging manner of telling stories will make you feel like you are having an intimate conversation with her. There are so many great nuggets, in this book, that you can use to recognize your blessings, align with God's plan and walk in your #GodCertification™.

Sonia Jackson Myles
Founder & CEO, The Sister Accord® LLC
Creator, Dreamwalking®

"There are never too many stories about the messy side of motherhood and women who face emotional challenges our mothers' generation didn't speak about. Andrea writes with vulnerability and openness that can help others to heal shame and sense of not-enoughness."

Tatiana "Tajci" Cameron
Music artist, speaker and coach

"Andrea is a determined wife, mother and follower of Jesus! She lays out a story that will inspire you to press on and trust the Lord even when life throws you curve balls. You'll find hope rising up in the pages of her testimony and see God's smile in the responses she shares to her challenges. Andrea puts her whole heart into her faith and trust in God's bigger plan for her life. God is surely to bless you through her story."

Shane Harden
Pastor - Branches Church, Columbus OH

Introduction

With clinched fists and red faces, the screaming begins, and the weight of his words clouds the air: *"I quit the family!"* And my response? *"Oh, no! Nobody quits the family before Momma, and Momma ain't quittin'!"* If my story were written out as a narrative, these quotes would be bold and bright red, blaring on the page.

Have you been there? In a moment when your struggle is blatantly throwing itself in your face and taking a victory lap? I certainly have! And it didn't help that I had puffed up my chest and dug in my boots for so long. In a defensive clamor, I knew there would be no surrender from the howling winds of this Momma's frustration.

Do you feel the sting of those moments that come from failure, the yearning to find yourself worthy of what you set out to do with all your heart? The anger of unmet expectations as well as the shock from unforgiving plot twists in life, all which seem to enjoy smearing ink across the lines of your family's story? For me, there was always something just out of reach, something I was unable to grasp. Something I knew would calm the chaos and silence the sound of that faint, ever-present laughter at my belief that I weaved a level of control throughout it all! It was like a soft wind blowing through the tops of the tree, moving its leaves delicately as they danced against the sky. I knew the wind was there. I could sense it all around me, yet it never brushed against my face. That laughter was born from pain, anxiety, and fear created by an unwanted, inappropriate childhood experience with an older boy at church, which I have kept secret for almost 40 years. That moment allowed a darkness to creep in and lay at the edges of my mind, waiting for an opportunity to overwhelm the words touching my life. Its hold over me caused destruction within my own heart and pain within the lives of those who cared about me.

What suffering is hidden within you now? What page of your story is so splattered with inkblots, the mere thought of it emerging terrifies your soul? What words are etched across your heart creating walls no one can scale? These are questions I asked myself as my story unfolded, exploded, and stalled—as I found myself being played by a character I barely recognized. I had to live through it to get through it, but I did emerge, and so can you!

The life I expected and the life I received have two very different narratives. When I was pregnant with my first child, I expected a perfect delivery with no complications and being able to bring home a healthy baby to a perfectly decorated new nursery. None of the ladies dishing out pregnancy stories and childhood advice had mentioned that my baby might be born not breathing, or that he could be diagnosed with a lifelong disability. Almost everything I thought I knew about having babies, and all of my expectations, were thrown out the window in the moment of our first son's birth. When you and your baby live through something traumatic like that, "life" takes on a whole new meaning! The same ladies also left out a lot about what was involved during the recovery from having a baby and the stresses of everyday motherhood. No one tells you what to do or how to function when you bring home a premature baby whose life was almost extinguished before it began. How do you prepare yourself for that moment or moments of such overwhelming disbelief when your kids are diagnosed further with Crohn's Disease, Attention Deficit Hyperactivity Disorder (ADHD), and separation anxiety? If you are me, you may start to think that plowing your car right over the mountainside seems to be the answer you seek because you just can't take one more punch to the gut. I felt robbed of my perfect childbirth experience those moms raved about, and on top of it all, I was unable to emotionally attach to my first child because of the birth trauma. I was spiraling down a cycle of fear. If becoming a mom is hard work, surviving it is even harder! Every day felt fragile and paper thin, like the ink trying to dry in order to solidify the words of my story could just drip right off the page with the frailest touch. I was exhausted from fighting, and I didn't even realize where I was living. I was living in what I call "the Quit," just trying to survive until given the precious opportunity to fully observe its impact around me, but we'll get to that later.

Where are you in your story? Still in the introduction? Halfway through? Are there edits you'd like to make? I'm here to tell you it's not too late. What I have learned along my journey has produced shifts for new ways of thinking and opportunities to connect with those around me in a more authentic way, opening new chapters beyond the measure of joy I thought I could know in my marriage and as a mom. You can find a new level of relationship with your spouse and kids if you can reach a place within your story that life is trying to keep hidden from you. That place you are seeking where you want to live because it answers the questions you have. But . . . you're going to have to do the work to uncover it!

If I'd had my way, I would've written a much calmer and comforting story for my family. I would have spared my kids the pain I felt they experienced by having me as their mother. I would've edited out the gut-wrenching blows of life-altering medical diagnoses for my kids, and I would have given each of them the journey I had planned for their lives with peace and without heartache, pain, or major challenges to overcome. In doing so, however, I would have ruined their growth and stagnated their potential that God had planned for them, not to mention their opportunities to walk out their purpose, as well as I'd have ruined mine. It took a very long time for me realize that through the disappointments, emotional devastation, and isolation I was experiencing, I was being prepared to endure the story of what was to come.

Being a mom, you learn to be flexible. It's required. But even so, I struggled with allowing God to be the author of my family's story. Our life was nothing like what we wished for, but it was everything God planned and knew we needed! I can tell you that by the time you reach the end of my story, you will have laughed, cried, and possibly peed a little from the tales I share! You will experience what it takes to stop fear from directing your path, how to stop living in the Quit, and how to recognize that each page of your story, no matter how tattered, stained, or crumpled, nor how much darkness is weaved throughout, is all required! You will find along the way that the purging of your story that you wish would take place can't be separated from the masterpiece God is creating in you. If it were, you would lose the beauty of those pages that define your authenticity. You may walk, run, and even crawl through your story, but It. Is. Yours! It's in these little moments you discover in the binding and margins that you realize growth is required to move forward, change is inevitable, and you can truly see what's holding you together and what's waiting on the other side!

I am Andrea Holman, singer, songwriter, author, and the host of a nationally syndicated show, *Wake Up Take a Minute!*

I speak to women across the country, sharing stories about my hilarious and gut-wrenching experiences as a mom. It's not an easy story to bear, but I have a burden in my heart to share love and encouragement with others who may find themselves in similar situations (or who just want to get a good laugh in at my expense!). For twenty-three unwavering years, I've been the wife of Luke, whom I met dancing and immediately loved, and we created a brilliant rhythm to move throughout life together! Even though we aren't always on the same page of music, we have always found our beat again. I am Mom to four incredible, hilariously funny, and dangerous kids, each of which are beloved for their individuality and unique personalities. (Which, if I'm being honest, took me a little longer with one of them, just saying!) I am also the fur baby mom of two adorable pups, one of which is a fake therapy dog, and the other… Lord, we are pretty sure she hit every dumb branch in her family tree on the way down! But I sure do love that dog anyway! I have made almost every mistake you can in raising kiddos, and I'm not done yet! I have experienced the emotional trauma, the rip-your-heart-out moments, the anxiety, and the drama of being a mom, and I have learned how to take the "highs with the blows." My story is one of living *in* the Quit and *through* the Quit to discover my purposeful and very real story that's so worth truly living!

1
It's Exhausting Being in Control

I grew up in the small East Tennessee town of Dayton. We did have more than one stop light, but if you blinked twice, you still might miss it. In fact, our town was so small that when McDonald's came to town, we thought we had hit the map! What did eventually put us on the map, however, was a result of a history deeply rooted in fundamental Biblical teachings and the "good ole American Way."

Our sleepy little town became famous in July 1925 as the world watched The Scopes Trial (also called the "Monkey Trial," in which a high school teacher, John T. Scopes, was prosecuted for teaching Charles Darwin's theory of evolution. This new state law, The Butler Act, had just been passed four months earlier and forbade the teaching of the "evolution theory" in any state-funded educational establishment. Essentially, they were not allowed to teach any theory that denies the story of Divine Creation, as taught in the Bible. You were not going to tell this state's kids that people descended from monkeys. Period.

When this law was passed, the American Civil Liberties Union (ACLU) saw this as a challenge to the 1st Amendment, and essentially asked the question, "Any of y'all in Tennessee want to 'fess up to teaching this so that we can defend you and win?" Businessmen from Dayton got together and knowing the attention (and revenue) it would bring to the city, they persuaded 24-year-old John T. Scopes to agree to be the scapegoat. He was unsure whether he had ever actually taught evolution, but he was found guilty and fined $100. The verdict, however, was overturned on a technicality.

The Scopes Trial captured the attention of the world, and for eleven short days placed the State of Tennessee and the City of Dayton under a microscope! The ACLU had secured famed lawyer Clarence Darrow, the first lawyer to successfully use science as a defense strategy in a trial, while the prosecution hired three-time Democratic Presidential candidate and former United States Secretary of State, William Jennings Bryan—a self-proclaimed expert on the Bible. Big-time names for a tiny little town.

So, if the trial had been staged to put Dayton on the map... it worked! The actions of a few that day altered more than a town. It altered the education system for the nation, as this legal battle laid the framework which allowed the ACLU to win its case in the higher courts to include the teaching of evolution in schools.

We are unable to foresee how far-reaching the effects of our decisions will transmit. The smallest ripples can create crashing waves of influence around the world. I find it fitting that this small, once-invisible town with its fundamental dynamics provides the setting in which I was raised. God, Country, and Southern Hospitality were our live-and-die-by mottos! (In that order.)

My family was definitely a typical small town, Southern family. We were very active in school, sports, the community, and the local church where we attended. If the church doors were open, we didn't miss a service unless someone was sick, or we were out of town. With most of our extended family living in Kentucky and Ohio, our friends and fellow church members were our surrogate family.

My dad and mom found a small, three-bedroom brick ranch home in the perfect neighborhood outside the city. My Mom said the grass was as high as the roof line when they bought it. After Dad mowed the yard down to a respectable size, we moved in and started making memories. There was always something to do, even if it was playing with a stick in mud puddles after it rained. I loved living in the country surrounded by water and woods. This was a perfect place to raise a fully energetic, crazy child like me. I was wild from the minute my feet hit the ground in the morning 'til my head hit the pillow at night! There was lots of open space for me to run or ride my bike and a huge lake for me to swim! The wilderness was my world, and I got lost in it every day. There was one road in and one road out of where we lived, so we knew almost everyone in the area. My neighborhood was like my own secret place in the world where I could be me, run wild, explore, and learn about life.

Growing up, after we did our chores, we were allowed to run loose. We were usually called back three times a day: for lunch, dinner, and bedtime. We had the best clock keeper, too—my friend's mom, Mrs. Dorothy Fine. Everyone called her Dot. She was the neighborhood whistler! When she stepped out on the back deck of her house, pursed her lips together and placed two fingers just on the edge of her lips, what happened next was the loudest, most piercing whistle to ever reach your ears! The sound carried for what seemed like miles, and if you didn't hear it, that meant you were too far away... and you were in trouble. The sound of her whistle created an invisible barrier that surrounded us. It defined the area we were allowed to explore within our daily world, and that whistle saved me more than a few times from being late to the table!

When I wasn't inside the house, my time was spent running through the woods, swinging on the old tire swing, riding my bike, swimming, climbing trees, trying to break into the Boys Club House, and chasing squirrels. Of course, only the ones that didn't bite me!

I love animals, and I would bring home every half-dead animal I could find while out playing, telling my mom, "It followed me home. We can't let it die!" I had lots of "outside pets" when I was little. I remember when some of the boys on our street found a few kittens who happened to have found the doves they had shot and left outside in my dad's boat. They told me they were going to put those kittens in a bag and throw it in the lake! I couldn't get to my dad fast enough to tell him exactly what they planned to do—I wasn't big enough to stop them myself, but he was able to intervene and save them. It wasn't those kittens' fault the boys were too stupid or lazy, leaving their birds out for something to find and eat. The boys were upset with me, but I couldn't have cared less . . . I saved the animals that day! I had a bleeding heart. At one point, I wanted to be a veterinarian when I grew up but honestly, I couldn't handle the blood. That career path was a lost cause for me. I still love animals, and to this day, I pump the brakes every time a squirrel, chicken, or turtle tries to cross the road. I just can't help myself!

So yes, we were the quintessential small-town family who supported our hometown football team, went to the farmer's market, played musical instruments in the school band, and walked through the neighborhood waving at the neighbors. I even waved at the mean ones! We helped neighbors with yard work, even if they weren't sick, and brought cookies and hot chocolate to the mailman on really cold days. I really enjoyed helping others and putting a smile on their face. My friends and I spent our days going to school, doing homework, and breaking down the doors to run outside and play! Except on Wednesday evenings, because we were attending church.

From childhood, I was taught to love everyone and follow your heart where God calls you. I loved my little country church. It was the only church I knew, as we started attending there when I was a baby. It was my safe and trusted place as a kid, no different than how I felt about my home. It was where I learned about Jesus and His sacrifice and love for me, that it was through His grace I was able to have a relationship with God. It's where I decided to trust Him and open my heart to His love. I learned so much from visiting pastors who shared stories of their incredible lives and the personal circumstances God brought them through. They fascinated me and captured my imagination of what was possible with God in your life. In my own mind, I perceived them as warriors for good as they painted vivid scenes of experiences and shared the journeys of their relationship with God. My childhood pastor could ignite a flame in your heart for God just as easily as he preached a sermon. He was loved dearly, and I still remember how I felt his profound absence in my life when he moved away. I was privileged to be surrounded by pastors who loved God and lived a life focused on Him.

On the other hand, my pastor's wife was my Sunday School teacher, and she and I had a very different relationship, as well as very different views on how a young girl should behave. That, coupled with the fact that I suffered from ADHD and was not medicated, made me the prime suspect for any trouble that happened in her class. I was always in trouble, and her main problem was that she couldn't catch me! I was a runner, a climber, and much faster at anything she tried to do. I would go anywhere in the church, inside or outside, to get away from her if she started giving me a problem. I knew I would be in a lot of trouble with my dad and mom, so I had to fully commit to the end when I ran from her! Oh, the gray hairs I gave her! God bless her heart. After all these years, I am still in contact with that pastor and his wife, and we laugh at all the "Fun Times" I gave them.

My home church was your typical small-town church building. From the outside, it was a simple building with stark white paint suffocating its walls. Our church sign sat at the front, close to the road, with bold black letters staring out at the world to invite those driving by to join us. I climbed that sign as often as possible and would run along the top of the brick wall that lifted it high into the air. My last visit to that brick wall was due to me not sitting quietly in church, and I remember a quick spanking for good measure that took place as well!

As you enter the sanctuary from climbing the stairs, the church pews ran from back to front, stopping just short of the pulpit where the preacher stood during the sermons. I spent many hours kneeling at the pulpit praying for everything I felt was wrong with the world, for my family and friends, and for all I was concerned about in life. Many of my tears were shed there, as I prayed sometimes silently and sometimes loudly as I spoke to God.

Dad was a deacon for the church, and Mom was a member of the choir and the church secretary. We attended choir practice every Wednesday. It's where my love of music started. I remember watching her sing and listening to the harmonies emerging through the songs. The sound of music flowed through me, and I felt as if it were touching my soul. I was so inspired by the beautiful orchestration of the songs that I started writing music on my own. I remember one day, my brother found my song book and showed it to my mom. He was howling out loud laughing about a song I wrote called "My Bike." He said, "She wrote a song about her bike! Who would listen to that? It's so stupid?" Now, it was somewhat crudely written, but oddly enough, I believe it really sounded like "I Love My Lips" by Larry the Cucumber! I was definitely ahead of my time, since VeggieTales wouldn't be invented for quite a while. My Mom told my brother, "Well, you write about what you know, and that's what she knows." I was glad she defended my creativity, but I stopped writing after his unsolicited feedback. My inspiration fell short for some time after that. Nevertheless, a burning desire was lit in my soul for music, and it would never be quenched. I loved listening to various styles of music from rock 'n' roll to gospel to classical. Even to this day, music is the one thing that calms my mind and spirit, and I know it's due to the hymns that touched my soul as a child.

I also participated in every children's church play for Easter, Christmas, or any other special event they decided the kids should perform for. I remember in one, I played a lightning bug! In fact, I still have the photos of me in those green leotards with little antennas on my head! Looking back, they were actually pretty risqué to wear at a little country church. Maybe at any church for that matter, but I was so young, how could it matter . . . I made those leotards look good!

One of my favorite things to do was to climb the church pole outside. Yep! You heard me! Even my Baptism Day wasn't off limits for my shenanigans. Shortly after I jumped out of the baptism pool and into dry clothes, I was off! After a while, I guess my dad started to wonder where I was and went looking for me outside. I'm sure he could hear the chanting around the side of the church as he began to search for me. I saw his head peek around the corner as the kids below were urging me on! "Go, Go, Go!" When he looked up and discovered me almost at the top, in my cute little dress and black patent leather shoes with my ruffled panties showing through my leotards, it was a look of horror! I'm sure he was scared to death that I would fall to the concrete parking lot below and die on the same day I was baptized. But for me, it was exhilarating! I was always looking for the next most dangerous thing to do. I could hardly keep my feet on the ground long enough to be caught, let alone be disciplined most days!

Between climbing trees, church poles, and the refrigerator by the age of two to reach the medicine cabinet, I was constantly in motion. When I first became a parent, my mom told me a story about taking me to the doctor for a checkup. I was at the doctor's office, opening each drawer and cabinet to inspect, one after the other. The doctor stopped talking and said, "You know she has ADHD, right?" To which Mom replied, "No. She's just a very curious child"! The doctor clearly disagreed and suggested medication. My mom was determined to let me just be me, no matter what energy level that brought with it. It's not like it interfered horribly with my life. I did get in trouble at school and church, but I was learning and could pay attention, so Mom thought it best to let me be and see where I ended up.

I certainly was a very exciting kid to have at a birthday party, on your team during field day, or on a field trip to the great outdoors! They required two chaperons for me! It's a good thing that my mom was a stay-at-home CEO . . . I would have never been able to go anywhere! I do believe, however, that having untreated ADHD added to my nervous energy when I was younger—my mind raced constantly—and prodded me to seek further control. I was unaware of how these symptoms could be displayed in an individual as a kid, so I had no idea that a lot of my actions and behavior were due to this diagnosis. I just thought this was how everyone's mind worked. But later, it would all make sense.

Although most of the childhood moments I reflect on are happy ones, there are moments I wish never happened. One life-changing day, the second safest place I knew was shattered into pieces, and a shift happened within me causing an out-of-control spiral of fear to enter my mind. When I was around the age of eight, a teenage boy led me to a room in the church where he touched me inappropriately. I still remember walking up the stairs with him, my hand in his as my patent leather shoes fell softly against the carpet. At the top of the stairs, there was a small landing, and then you turned to enter the Sunday School rooms for all the young kids. I can recall walking through that door, the first one on the right, and the exact spot in the room he told me to lay down. I remember him talking to me like it was just any other day, as if there was nothing unusual about his actions. I didn't know to be afraid or scared of him; after all, I had known him my whole life. I didn't know what he was doing was wrong, but he did. At one point he stopped and walked close to the door to press his ear firmly against it because he thought someone was coming up the stairs. After he decided his time with me was over, we walked toward the door, and I walked out with him talking to me like nothing happened, and that's how I treated it. Like nothing happened.

At that point, how could I know that this would set me on a path into a need for controlling the narrative of my story and all circumstances around me? That it would overshadow my life as a woman, as a wife, and as a mother, as well as become a catalyst that would guide me through future decisions for years? My church and my little town were no longer safe.

There was a haze of darkness that clouded my mind. I was filled with confusion, pain, and the feeling of judgment because even though no one knew what had happened, I did. Life continued to move forward, but something was growing within my heart that would not stay buried.

My teen years were smooth and steady when viewed from the outside. Our town was peaceful and as slow paced as the lighting bugs floating around the yards at dusk. That McDonald's which we thought would put us on the map became a favorite hangout for the teens, and cruising cars around the parking lot became a real activity. Outside of hanging at the local Pizza Hut and family-owned movie theater (where the entire town congregated to watch Rocky IV, in which Rocky defeats the Soviet Union boxer Drago), this was where all the excitement took place in town.

Although there were rumors about bonfire parties out in the country where all the older teens hung out, we weren't allowed to attend any activity that wasn't sanctioned by the church. The closest thing I ever came to wild parties were the church skate nights at the local skating rink where they played upbeat music! I was skilled at roller skating, and I pushed those skates to the limit of the sound barrier as I was trying to outrun the sparkling lights of the disco ball hanging from the ceiling. Looking back on those nights skating, I remember how free I felt. Like I could almost fly away on those skates. How I wished I could outrun that town in hopes that one day, it would all become a blank invisible page in my story.

As a child imagining your future, you can't predict how your experiences or the people you encounter will create conflict or interfere with your life later. As I passed through my teenage and young adult years, I made countless decisions with negative and positive outcomes. Some of which I definitely knew were wrong; however, at the time I didn't care because it felt like the right decision. Some shaped me in positive ways, encouraged and built me up, while others tried to extinguish the faint remaining light I had concealed within the crevasses of my heart.

The older I became, the stronger my storms grew within, bringing with them much higher levels of destruction as I experienced the vast world around me. I wasn't going to let anyone tell me what to do, not even my dad. We had more than a few heated arguments about my behavior, and I held my ground at all costs. I pushed him away the most, and I threw a lot of my pain into that relationship. In my young adult life while dating, if anyone tried to get too close physically, they were in for a full-on fight. After my childhood experience, I didn't ask twice for someone to stop doing something, even if they were holding my hand too tightly; it triggered to me that you were trying to control me, and that I was vulnerable in some way. I didn't know that my reactions weren't normal;

they were just how I shielded myself from unwanted attention or probing questions. My desire to remain disconnected emotionally was especially guarded. I clung to a level of controlled anger lurking just beneath the surface waiting to engulf anyone who threatened to crack through.

You know, when you have a life-altering experience touch your life, creating valleys of deep wounds that need to mend, it's difficult to recognize where you begin and where the wounds should end. Even within my most fragile moments, when I had opportunities to be authentic, I still was unable to give life to those words that created my pain. I just recoiled and went back to being a spectator of my own life, being protective of my family, judging myself and the actions taken to reach that point. I lost myself in the storms that raged within me, and sometimes they threatened to wash away all my efforts to camouflage the layered protective realm of control I worked to wield. That realm of control, even though it wasn't real, felt real enough and allowed me the ability to distance myself from situations even within my mind, creating a barrier for emotions to hide. There were times, though, when all you had to do was look at me the wrong way and you were left feeling the sting of my words across your heart. I was especially protective of my little sister growing up, after what happened to me. I was so protective, in fact, that when I was sixteen years old, I confronted a man who could not control his eyes from roaming across her body—with his wife walking next to him, by the way! When I felt vulnerable or threatened, I was ruthless in my language and crafty with my attacks.

I had plenty of reasons in my mind not to seek healing. As a child, I had no ability to explore the damage that was created in my life at church that day. As I grew older, the fear, anxiety, vulnerability, embarrassment, pain, and—quite frankly—an unwillingness to release my realm of control to deal with all my emotional baggage, deterred me from investigating real healing. I wasn't about to give up the façade which I had fought so hard to build.

It took a long time for me to realize that through the pain I was experiencing, I was being prepared to endure what was to come. Believe me, I could have never anticipated the lessons ready to fall across the pages of my life! Turns out, I needed to seek after and hold tight to the God who I gave my heart to all those years ago as a child in a small-town church! I had to let myself be vulnerable. I had to relinquish control. Yes, I knew He loved me, but I was so wounded and lost, with a heart so scribbled on, that it was difficult seeking Him, let alone clinging to Him. Usually when we seek and cling to God, it is when the storm threatens to swallow us whole, when there's nothing else left to do but grab for Him and hold on tight. He is the calm and the peace we need in the eye of the storm. If we will reach for Him.

Becoming vulnerable is essential, though it certainly doesn't come easy or make this girl feel good. I spent years soul searching, in therapy, (finally) taking medication, and praying, and do you know what I learned? My control, fear, and anxiety were never mine to carry! I found that I could only find myself by releasing my truth out into the universe. Once I understood that pursuing the real Me would set me free, it changed my perspective, as well as my emotional and spiritual focus.

I'm not the true version of who I'm supposed to be just yet, but I know she's there because I recognize her in the quiet. I'll catch a glimpse of her in my kids' smiles or in the twinkle in their eyes. My story is unfolding a little more every day while new storms are accumulating to emerge on the horizon. However, continuing to release control generates new strength to survive the challenges of a twenty-three-year marriage and being Momma to four incredible, hilariously funny, and downright dangerous kids! I'm not going to sugar coat it y'all, marriage and motherhood have both proven to be overwhelming at times! There have been moments in which the notion of whether I'd survive it all crept into the margins of my story.

But I know now that I was my own worst enemy, sabotaging my own happiness until I finally figured out that I had to relinquish the illusion of control to fully live. I couldn't hold on to it anymore; because y'all, it's exhausting being in control!

2
40 Weeks of Pregnancy?

As I grew into a young lady, my imagination explored the possibilities of who I would become. Years of my life would pass before thoughts of having kiddos would cross my mind. I knew I wanted kids and marriage someday, but I just wasn't sure when that would fit into my future life of swimming with dolphins. As a buck wild, water-loving kid obsessed with animals, I decided that working as a marine biologist would definitely be the coolest career in the whole wide world. I didn't know what it would take to get there, but that was what I was going to be! How were kids and a husband going to fit on a boat with me and with all my work stuff?

I also remember overhearing the ladies at church talk about what a "blessing" their babies were. Of course, by overhearing, I mean I was totally eavesdropping on their conversations. I could sneak up on anyone while in stealth mode, and they would never know I was there. Then during church, I would see those same ladies throw blazing glares across the church pews at their kids when they acted up! Those looks sure didn't convey a feeling of "blessedness" to me . . . Just saying!

What did I know, though? I was just a kid! I was around babies my whole life, so I watched as the ladies took care of them. It didn't seem like it was such hard work to me: You feed them a bottle, burp them, change their diapers, change their clothes, lay them down for a nap, and repeat! Nothing to this baby thing, right? I thought I knew it all when I was young, and I believed I was invincible! I thought nothing could shake my core or break me down. Of course, looking back, I'm glad for my blissful bout of ignorance while it lasted. I'm sure if I knew then what I know now about raising children, I couldn't have seen myself as a mom. This stuff's hard, y'all! Really hard!

I know now what it feels like to have your heart ripped out, thrown to the floor, and cut into tiny pieces every time your kid is given a life-altering diagnosis. That you feel helpless when your body is literally ripped apart, and you're only able to offer prayers, knowing your child might die while entering this world. That there's a cold, deafening isolation after becoming a mom—even though you are surrounded by loved ones—along with a nagging feeling you are not worthy to have the title. I know that it feels like the prick of a sharp knife when you hear the first, "I Hate You!" escape from lips that he inherited from you! However, worst yet, I know the feeling of crippling devastation, of your heart going numb as anger rises when you have failed to protect a child from the lurking evil of this world. Becoming their mom has left my heart exposed, unraveled, and wounded repeatedly; but there is also great joy, wonder, and abundant love written through it all. I was not prepared for the unexpected experiences I would face being a mom, and I must say they exposed my vulnerabilities rather quickly and ignited my "fight or flight" response. I'm going to tell you right now, there's not a whole lot of "flight" in this girl, so we were definitely going to see trouble! Prepare yourselves, future mommas, because the battle begins well before those babies arrive!

I remember when I was around seventeen, my older sister was expecting her first baby. She had a difficult pregnancy with horrible morning sickness. She stated all the time it would be her only child, and she wasn't lying! As I recall her pregnancy, that portion wasn't what I was focused on. It was the hardship of her delivery, which ended in an emergency C-section! The stories she shared just did me in and terrified me, and I was absolutely positive I would not be experiencing *that* when I delivered my babies.

I met my husband Luke at the age of twenty-three, and once we knew we were going to be married, we devised a plan to have kiddos early in marriage. God allowed him to enter my life at the place where you could find me every Friday and Saturday night—a local dance club! I'm so thankful that God will meet us where we are. Even through all my poor decisions and stubbornness, God still chose to bless me with Luke. He was the answer to my prayers, and even though

I hated the wait, God's timing was perfect. I was ready to meet who God wanted in my life, and that made all the difference! As we discussed what our future life would look like, we wanted to be those young, forty-year-old adults who were able to travel because we'd had our kids early in marriage and they were out of the house! It mostly worked out—we were partially delayed due to having a few more kids than we originally planned. Each one of our kids was just so cute! I couldn't help myself!

When it came to the number of kids, we really just wanted healthy babies. I knew I did not want only one, as I worried an only child could carry all the weight of his or her parents' expectations to achieve great things in life, which could cause a great deal of stress for the child. Also, I can't imagine being an only child and losing your parents and not having siblings to lean on for comfort. I come from a family of four, and Luke has one sibling. I also didn't want to have just two kids because I was afraid they may not like each other! I mean, it can happen. I've seen family drama where the two kids don't get along, and it grows into a poisonous relationship that lasts into adulthood, as well as divides a marriage. Although this can certainly happen with any number of kids due to their personalities, I was convinced that three or four would be a good number. We decided to move forward with our family pretty quickly after marriage so we could achieve our timeline!

I can't tell you how many other moms I have met who, as we share our battle scars, say to me, "Where was the chapter on this when I was expecting?" or "Why didn't they cover that during pregnancy classes?" or "No one explained what to do with a child who screams twenty-four hours a day, seven days a week and won't sleep!" No one told me anything about the ugly side of pregnancy, delivery, or raising kids, and I've found that most of us feel like we were unprepared for the forty weeks of pregnancy, let alone the aftermath of the delivery and shifting into motherhood! I certainly know I wasn't.

Each mom has a very unique experience, because no two adoptions, births, or deliveries are alike. However, we share similar heart stories, feelings, and moments along the way. I am sure that I am not the only mother—although I felt like it at the time—who was shocked or disgusted with my thoughts toward others during hormonal rage, exhausted from all the work involved in pregnancy, or totally mortified after entering what I called "lunatic mode" when someone made a comment I found offensive! (God help them and *bless their hearts*!) Needless to say, my extra hormones usually worked against me throughout my pregnancies.

As moms, we are expected pretty much to wear a smile, even through the exhaustion, pain, and that strange waddling effect that happens when your body contains a small human! Not to mention all those times we are required to contain a small toddler ready to blow their lid with just a toothpick, dental floss, and some sticky tape! Oh wait, that's MacGyver! We carry a lot of burdens, as well as badges of honor. I'll tell you right now, becoming pregnant and giving birth does not a Momma make. Biologically, yes; however, there is a lot more to being a mother than just giving birth. For some, becoming a mom takes a long journey; like a rare comet that flashes across the sky, emerging once every hundred years. While for others, it seems to come swiftly as a shooting star falling to earth's atmosphere.

Before you even arrive at the forty-week wait, you've long begun the journey to motherhood. There is an entire life lived prior to the pregnancy! I always found it funny that I never noticed a pregnant woman until I wanted a child. Then, I swear it seemed like every woman of child-bearing age who passed me on the street was pregnant! Where did they all come from? They were always there. It's just like everything else in life; you don't notice something until it affects you directly. Until then, it had blended in with the world around you seamlessly.

I spent years in self-doubt and fear after my first almost-forty-weeks. Our first son arrived early, so I didn't feel the full effects of late pregnancy. We have four kiddos, and we experienced two miscarriages, as well. I still think about my little babies and carry that loss and pain. There is a lot more to this pregnancy thing than anyone ever divulges, and there are so many complications that can occur. It's like skiing downhill—when one ski falls off, the other one slants left, and your body turns right! I faced many challenges each step of the way. First, you must get pregnant. Then you must stay pregnant. Then, once you've managed to stay pregnant, you must prepare yourself, your spouse, and your house and vehicles for the arrival which, if you're lucky, is close to the date you were told! I'm a complete Type A personality . . . a big-time planner. However, I found that babies just don't comprehend directions well or typically operate within the restrictions of our plans. What brats they can be! I mean seriously, I only asked for a little cooperation!

My first pregnancy took us seven months, me quitting school, selling and buying a home, plus a business trip to Canada to make happen! All in all, I was anxious over the amount of effort required to create new life! I mean, God created the entire world in seven days. I was just trying to fertilize an egg here! How hard could it be?

Luke and I were literally in the middle of selling our first house in Cincinnati, Ohio, when, three days into showings, our air conditioning went out. In summer. It's hard to keep cool when there is no air circulating through the house. The oppressive heat started to match the oppressive emptiness I felt within my unoccupied uterus! Yep, that's how it goes. You make a plan, and life throws distressing challenges at your doorstep!

After weeks of showings, we sold the house just in time, as we found a great house that was perfect for our (hopefully) growing family. We had sold and purchased a new home all within weeks, and in the middle of that chaos, I was called away to Canada on a business trip. I vividly remember because not only was it during the worst possible time personally, but while traveling I found myself alone in a hotel room realizing I indeed was not pregnant. Again, I was a failure. I placed a trembling hand on the phone to call Luke that night. As my heart sank sharing the news, I could hear his voice always encouraging and loving even through the physical distance. I didn't know how much more disappointment I could take. Even though, according to the doctors' timelines, we had barely been trying long enough to count since they don't consider you having issues until you reach around two years of trying without results.

I returned home—with a heaviness on me—to moving box chaos. It was so busy and exhausting. We were packing boxes, taping boxes, loading boxes, moving boxes, unloading boxes, and unpacking boxes! I was in hustle mode, planning, organizing, and trying to get everything finished by the deadlines. By the time we moved to the new house, roughly a month later, I'd seen enough boxes and I never wanted to touch another one again—unless it contained a pregnancy test, of course. We had packed those, too! And it was just a few days prior to the actual move when we found ourselves in need of them . . .

You can imagine our surprise and the excited, joyous buzz we felt we had to share! A huge weight in my heart was lifted when I saw those two lines streak across the pregnancy test window. I could hardly believe it because we were so focused on moving, we weren't discussing anything about a baby. There were tears, laughter, hugs, and more tears. I was already fantasizing how to decorate his room, planning the shower dates, and thinking of names! Excitement was sure to fill the upcoming months as we anxiously waited to meet our new baby.

I'm going to share a secret with you that I discovered. Are you ready? Here we go: I have learned throughout each of my pregnancies that there were a lot of things others left out or forget to mention about welcoming a child into the world. Whether by accident or on purpose, I'm not sure. However, looking back on my six pregnancies, there do seem to be a few things I can't recall. So, maybe we do indeed forget.

Others certainly remember to share the joy of watching their bodies change with a sweet, growing baby bump. They remember to tell you about the excitement of baby showers thrown by loved ones with congratulatory hugs from everyone as they touch your belly, giggling and guessing the real birth date, weight, and length of your sweet baby! They recall how magical it feels knowing that a new tiny life is growing inside of their amazing body. How their skin glows from motherhood, and that their hair is silkier than it's ever been. Of course, they'll remember that there were some aches and pains and an experience of slight morning sickness occasionally, but no big deal—you can certainly manage those small inconveniences. After all, any hardship is forgotten once you're past the smooth delivery, during which the epidural works perfectly, and at the end of all your efforts you are rewarded with a curly headed bundle of joy who latches on properly and starts to nurse right away.

Yeah! That's what I envisioned too. And it's a beautiful, thoughtful scene. It's just not what happened for me.

I, too, experienced some of those exciting thrills along the way. However, I'm pretty sure that no one could have equipped me for my first forty weeks! My first trimester included, but was not limited to, hanging my head into the best toilet option I could find at work while throwing up my lunch—every single day. Also, because I often threw up breakfast on the way to work, all over the car's dash during the morning drive, I couldn't wait to get rid of that car. Whoever has it now . . . sorry! After the first trimester, I settled into the second with mostly normal activities like continuing to gain weight while getting regular blood draws and ultrasounds.

Our first ultrasound was amazing. As I laid on the table, we watched at first what looked like a blob laying perfectly still.

The technician was like, "See your little baby"? Nope lady, we really don't know what we are looking at! She started to explain the images as the device rolled around on my belly, and pretty soon, we were able to see our son! He was an active little guy, bouncing all around in utero. Once they had confirmed he was a boy, they continued the procedure showing his little hands, feet, and the size of his head, as well as capturing the little flutter of his heart as he was cradled safely in his home. First, seeing him was one of the most tender moments, followed by the most memorable—he waved at us! He actually waved! At us! Even the technician was shocked, and we all started laughing! We couldn't believe that in a few short months we would welcome this new little guy into our life. We knew things would change, but we were young, and we could handle whatever was thrown our way.

I was so glad for that precious, memorable moment with him because it would bring comfort later during my ongoing struggle to stay pregnant. Months of medicine, shots, and bed rest thrown in just for good measure began halfway through my second trimester. My self-worth started to decline along with my failing body. It was like a tiny snowball rolling downhill, gaining momentum as my body initiated a pregnancy protest presented as full-blown, pre-term labor! I felt such isolation and devastation start creeping into the corners of my mind. Thoughts continued repeatedly that I had failed at providing safety for my little son. I started second-guessing every decision

I made and was overwhelmed by the onslaught of medical treatments and the bed rest regimen I was assigned. Being a Type A personality, this was not working out well with my birth plan or my life plan! I was upset, anxious, and honestly, mad! All the while, I was putting on a smile and acting like I had it all together, as if my heartache weren't crushing me with every one of my baby's heartbeats.

Clearly not everyone has experienced a difficult pregnancy or delivery. The difficulties we do encounter along the journey are also hard to discuss, as those who struggle carry a sense of shame to some extent. I know I did. When, in all actuality, we are some *Bad Sass Mommas*! I know I carried a sense of shame for many years until I was able to work through the trauma of my pregnancies, miscarriages, and deliveries. You never know how things will transpire when you begin trying to grow your family. We believe whole heartedly that our pregnancy will be on point with no troubles. But, just sometimes, that old saying of "no pain, no gain" comes into play, and things can go really awry.

I didn't wake up around 5:30 a.m. on March 13th, 2000 (finally out of my second trimester, but with weeks to go), expecting my life to unravel like a pretty bow you open on a baby shower gift, but it sure did. It didn't look so pretty afterward, either. It would take forty-four hours, multiple trips to the hospital, and ninety seconds to change our lives indefinitely, forevermore.

I awoke to a harsh and uncomfortable pressure growing in my back and radiating around my sides. I knew there was something happening because the pain was awful. I expected stomach labor pains, but no one ever mentioned back labor pain! This was unexpected and suffocating pain as it progressed.

I made my way carefully out of the bed in an effort not to disturb my sleeping husband, who was loudly snoring next to me. I waddled down the stairs and into the living room to lay on the couch. The pain continued to grow, and no position I tried changed a thing. At one point, I walked over to the corner of the walls and pressed the edge as hard as I could against it, trying to get some relief. I even placed a tennis ball on the wall, using it to massage my back, to no avail. I finally ended up kneeling on the floor next to the couch, arching my back and placing pillows under my belly for support. That worked for a little while, until it didn't! I quickly realized at that point, that something just didn't seem right about the pain, and we needed to call the doctor. I walked up the stairs to wake up my husband from his sweet slumber with a not-so-sweet "Honey! Wake UP!" We talked to the doctor and then drove to the hospital. We arrived relatively quickly, and they immediately started sticking needles and cords all over me.

At one point throughout the day, the sweet little ultrasound technician made the mistake of gently suggesting that according to the measurements, I was going to have a healthy, seven-and-a-half-pound baby. Now, some women may have appreciated that little tidbit of information, but in no such way did I! I sharply cranked my neck around to look her dead in the eye and set her straight! Through gritted teeth, I practically growled that she had lost her ever-loving mind, and that "Nothing THAT big is coming out of MY body!"

She may have seen that look before in an expectant mother's eyes, but something told me she had never had someone say that to her! Thank God, she granted me some grace and flashed a sweet smile. I was out of my mind already with the stress of this baby trying to leave his residence prematurely, and I couldn't handle anything else that wasn't going according to my birthing plan! I was going to have a normal delivery, with a healthy *little* baby boy, who would enter the world weighing in close to the threshold of six pounds if it was the last thing I did! Oh, to be young and naive, thinking I had any control over it. Ignorance is such bliss!

Through the course of the day, I was sent home a couple of times due to lack of activity and delivery progression. They felt that even though I was in horrible pain, there was nothing definitive happening at a speed with which they could justify keeping me. I begged to differ, but honestly, I was so exhausted from lack of sleep and fighting the pain that I couldn't bring myself to argue. At some point, later in the evening (or early morning for all I know), we went back to the hospital, and they decided to admit me. It would take hours of labor pain, a host of interns and nurses, physical exams, and what seemed like every doctor in the hospital using their tricks to keep my labor from progressing. I was only thirty-five weeks pregnant, after all! Unfortunately, my son's birth didn't turn out the way anyone expected . . . especially me!

Life isn't always sunshine and rainbows. You can't plan for something you have no control over, and here was the ugly straight truth that day—my baby boy was rattling the cage and working to break out early! I'm talking five-and-a-half weeks early, and we were in a very serious situation! The reality was that my doctor had been trying to stop my preterm labor for months prior to this episode, and we knew that I would probably not make it full-term with the pregnancy. My body was exhausted from fighting with itself to provide a safe haven for our baby, and I felt like a pin cushion from all the shots I had received to help him develop in case he was born early. Trying to prevent what was happening that day was the reason I had been medicated and confined to bed rest for months—all to allow my son to fully develop before my body served an early eviction notice. And now, we were working against a clock that was spinning out of control.

That's where we found ourselves during my delivery. After realizing my body was uncooperative to subdue the delivery, the doctors decided to move forward with inducing labor. They tried everything to help my delivery along. They broke my water, gave me Pitocin to increase contractions and had me constantly moving to uncomfortable positions or walking. If I could have done a "jig with a pig" to make it work, I would have! Literally, anything was an option as far as I was concerned, but nothing progressed my labor. The worst part of it all? My cervix had only dilated two centimeters after all those hours of being in the hospital! Talk about being aggravated!

Oh, and did I mention that I gave birth during a full moon and the worst springtime blizzard anyone had seen in years? Now, you're probably thinking, what does a full moon or blizzard have to do with anything? That's what we thought, too! Evidently, the full moon is when all the craziness hits the hospital. Anything that can go wrong or doesn't usually happen, happens. The blizzard complicates the hospital emergency staffing and compounds anything else that could go wrong when roads ice over.

The chatter from the nurses was all about the craziness swirling through the maternity ward! Every bed was filled with ladies in labor, and it just so happened that I arrived the same day that three sets of twins were being delivered. Three sets! Now, usually that wouldn't be a big deal, however; when you have a patient (hint, like me) who suddenly needs an emergency C-section, and both surgical units are occupied delivering twins, you have a problem.

At this point, the situation developed into my worst nightmare. The doctors were watching both my son and me closely, and he had entered a period of distress. The doctor told us that our son's heartrate was dropping, and that the situation was becoming more dire. This announcement made my very skin crawl! I knew exactly what she was saying, and I knew the words I spent my entire pregnancy trying to avoid were going to escape her lips and chill the air. A wave of sickness released over my body as she matter-of-factly stated, "We need to perform a C-section. Your labor is not progressing. His heart rate and oxygen levels continue fluctuating. We need to deliver him soon." Up until that point I liked her very much.

Seriously, a C-section! Sweet Jesus! My mind was racing with thoughts and questions. How did it come to this? Why did it come to this? Why can't I just be normal and birth a baby like everyone else? I was terrified! I wanted to scream at the top of my lungs! Everything in me panicked, and then there was nothing. That's when I think it started. I began to descend into a void and shut my emotions down, because I knew I couldn't think about what was going to happen, or I would flip totally out! I had to distance myself from the horribleness of it all. I didn't want to hear about it or discuss it. I wanted everyone and everything to just disappear, for that one moment to be frozen in time without any sound.

The next few hours passed with bodies moving in and out of my room, as well as with continual exams. We were told there were multiple deliveries before us so it would take a little longer to get me to the operating room. (Remember those sets of twins that all needed to be rushed in for delivery?) By now, our extended families had been at the hospital for hours waiting for our precious son's arrival. We told them that since it was still going to be a while for the surgery, they should all go eat. I knew if my dad didn't eat soon, he would become sick from the stress, so I was grateful he agreed to go. It wasn't long after they left the hospital, however, that things started heading south!

Our son's situation began to reach a critical point. Not only had my body been trying to evict him the past two months, but he was currently filing a grievance and fighting while we were trying to serve the papers! He was struggling inside of me. We had no idea at that time what he was really going through inside, and we wouldn't start grasping that until he turned fifteen months old.

We were in a holding pattern on the runway, waiting for my turn to be ushered through the swinging operation room doors so we could start the procedure. It was close to 8 p.m. when my bed headed down the hallway, and Luke was left to get dressed for his upcoming debut as a new daddy. Our families had not returned to the hospital yet, but this was it.

We were handing in the tickets and boarding the plane! Only this ride would take off the runway quickly, with no brakes, fastened seat belts, or flotation devices nearby.

The door swung open, and they rolled me into the operation room; there was a chill in the air. I remember the doors swinging closed behind me as my bed came to rest next to the table where I would be cut open very shortly. I was trying to focus on anything but the fact that I would be laying on that cold, sterile-looking table soon, but the anxiety was building inside of me. The lights were so bright shining down over the table, and there were a lot more people in the room than I expected. Two teams, in fact, were required for this event. One for me, and one to care for our son when he blessed the world with his arrival.

The nurse was checking all the tubes plugged into my body, and the anesthesia doctor was speaking to me about the epidural he had placed earlier in the day. I heard a lot of noise and chattering at the end of the table, but I refused to look for fear I might see the surgical instruments being prepared. I remember feeling like I was going to throw up as I laid in my hospital bed, waiting. Before I knew it, I was moving through the air and being laid gently on the cold, steel table, its touch chilling me to the bone, and then suddenly everything went from bad to worse…

I heard my doctor say, "Get him out! Get him out now!" My baby's heartrate had bottomed out, and they had lost him. He was gone; no movement and no sound coming from the machines. I looked up and saw the reflection of the doctors in the metal encasement surrounding the light above. She moved her hand over my stomach, rested the knife on my lower belly, and pressed down hard, cutting deeply through my skin. I looked away at the first sight of blood. A few moments later, I snuck a peek only to see her hands inside me, and I again turned my head away, deciding I didn't want to see what happened next! It was all happening so fast. I felt the pulling and tugging as my body was split open in the only way they could save our son. I was moving on the table, as there had been no time to tie my arms down for additional stability through the procedure. I remember thinking for a fleeting moment, *Luke's not even with me and they will never allow him into this chaos*, because this was now an emergency situation. They were trying to save my baby's life, and every second counted.

The room seemed colder now, and time stood still. I could feel my heartbeat quicken as the anticipation continued to build for this nightmare to be over! There was a quietness within the storm. Somehow those horrific moments were frozen in time, searing each scene into my mind. What seemed like an eternity later, Luke appeared next to me with the biggest grin on his face as any eagerly expecting father would wear prior to meeting his son. He had no idea how emergent the situation had become. As he reached over to hold my hand, bruised from all the IVs, I locked eyes with him and said, "This isn't normal. He's not breathing. He's NOT BREATHING!" Luke said, "He's OK. He's fine." My voice raised as I told him again, "No. he's not!" And mere moments later, our first child was born, blue and unmoving, not screaming…and not breathing. In fact, it was exactly ninety seconds from the first knife impression on my belly to when he was yanked into this world, and those ninety seconds changed our lives forever.

As they pulled him out of my belly, they realized the cord was wrapped twice very deeply around his neck. I could see their hands feverishly working to untangle the cord as I looked in the light rim above the bed. His body was limp as they hoisted him into the air and quickly rushed to the doctors and nurses waiting to look him over. I remember at this point, glancing at Luke and he had stopped smiling; his face was drawn and taut as he realized the gravity of the situation we were now facing. I never heard Cameron cry.

I remember hearing muffled voices as I glanced over to look for Cameron. I couldn't see him, and I didn't want to hear what the doctors were saying. Finally, a nurse spoke close to my head, and I turned, coming face to face with our son as the nurse held him close. Thank God, he was breathing. I knew that little fluttering heart beat we had seen on the ultrasound was still beating! I remember how soft he felt for the briefest of moments as I pressed my lips against his face and inhaled his scent. Right after that, he was whisked away to the Neonatal Intensive Care Unit (NICU) for monitoring. I don't remember much of what happened after that except I started to scream, "No! No! No!" I was told later that after Cameron was taken from the operating room, I started to panic on the doctors as they were working on me. They had to sedate me so they could safely finish my procedure.

I woke up to see Luke standing by my bed and both our moms in the room. He was explaining some of the complications that took place during surgery and the horrifying experience of almost losing Cameron. Their faces were white with shock as his words settled on the air. A little while later, I recall seeing each one of my family members' faces, each more stricken than the next, as nurses wheeled my bed down the hall toward the NICU. They realized how close we had come to losing our little guy, as well as the strain of what happened to me. In the NICU, they parked me at the base of Cameron's feet, and all I could see were his ten little beautiful toes. His face was mostly hidden from view, but I could read his nametag and all the miraculous details about him. Wouldn't you know it, he only weighed five pounds and eight ounces! I knew nothing bigger than six pounds was being delivered from my body! I reached my shaking hand up and extended a finger to softly brush the bottom of his foot. His skin was soft, and he felt wonderful. I was elated that the delivery was over. He was here. He was breathing. We had both made it through. There was still a long recovery ahead, but now that we were both safe, I could focus on healing and taking on the new role of Momma!

Absent during the delivery of his first grandchild was my father-in-law, Mark. He wasn't even in the country! Why, you may ask? Well, he was on a dive trip in the middle of the ocean. It had been planned months ago, when there had been no reason to believe that I would go into labor that early. My mother-in-law sent a fax to the boat, and over dinner that night the captain of the ship announced he was a new grandpa! Mark was so excited and overcome with joy! We found out later that the dive site where he was diving while Cameron was being born was named "God's Thumb." Do you think that was an accident? I don't. God's hand was on Cameron's life during every moment. From the time he was conceived to when he died and to the very moment God granted him back to us, God was cradling him in His mighty, powerful hands. We witnessed the most terrifying and marvelous moments during those two days. Everything had to be flawless within God's plan for the outcome to be achieved. If for some reason we had any doubt whether God set in motion all the actions of the day or were worried the details of our lives were too small for Him to notice, the dive location where Mark floated below the ocean waves during our experience was proof that we were in His loving grasp, right under His thumb, the entire time.

There are many things I have learned through each of my pregnancies, and it took years for me to become prolific in understanding and applying them. Sometimes I would forget, and the lesson was required again, which I must say was very irritating! I've learned that encountering unexpected hardships, failures, joys, and accomplishments along the way is inevitable, but it's my choice how I let them affect me. I get to choose to carry them or to let them go.

I wish I would have grasped this knowledge earlier and learned how to control my reactions faster. I had my entire pregnancies planned out. I will openly tell you, this was not a good idea! No one can fully prepare for the changes you encounter through a pregnancy. It's a very personal journey, and no two are the same! I had a very specific written-out plan, with timelines, to-do lists and a Plan B just in case my original plan had to be tweaked! My only problem was that I based this plan around a pregnancy I had absolutely no control over, but you couldn't tell me that. There was no way for me to impose my will on God's plan, no matter how well-thought-out the plans were or how strong-willed I was. By chiseling my plans out as if they were written in stone, all I did was create feelings of incompetence in my heart when my pictured delivery failed to come to fruition. I carried this self-loathing, silent pain with me for years, until I was reminded that walking by faith was my only hope through it. Later, when Cameron was diagnosed with Cerebral Palsy (CP), again I blamed myself because I felt that I let him down as a mom, even though I really was never in control. God had already accounted for every moment and each detail of that day, and God's plan prevailed. I can't say I understand each part of it, but I know that God's hand was on Cameron the entire time and in those moments of my seemingly horrific failure, God was creating a uniquely qualified person to live out his purpose according to God's plan. Not mine.

"Be You, 'Cause I'm Taken!" I have coined this phrase, which conveys a weighted, authentic truth, and I love it! Each of us has different gifts, talents, and experiences to draw from and impart to those around us. Your family needs and deserves an authentic, healthy *You*! So, *do You*! There have been many moments in my life during which the noise around me was deafening, overwhelming, and confusing for long periods of time. Looking back, I wish I had taken time to be more focused and homed in on God during these times. If I had taken the time sooner to explore who I really was, allowing God to fully have control in my life, I believe I could have accepted the authentic *Me* sooner. But I had to go through the pain, sorrow, joy, and experiences so I could appreciate the work it took to become my authentic self. There are reasons why you can't teach your kids everything you know, because some lessons must be learned on your own, no matter how many times it takes. It's worth it, and you are worth it, too! Focus on God's plan, hone in on your gifts, be open to new paths along the journey, and don't give up! I'm not a warrior because I win all the time. I'm a warrior because I always fight! No matter how long it takes, keep fighting until you can be *You*! Because everyone else is taken!

It's crazy how numbers seem to dictate much of life as we know it. We use math every day for formulas and calculations we do quickly in our heads without even knowing it. Even though I hated math in school, I know that numbers are important. Numbers hold value for critical moments in our life: birthdays, wedding anniversaries, and celebrations all around the world take place on specific dates to honor their level of importance. Then there are the numbers ingrained in my mind for those heartbreaking moments, as well: anniversaries of deaths, injuries, broken hearts, and so many other losses. The list goes on and on.

I can tell you two critical numbers in my life I will never forget. The first is thirty-five-and-a-half. This is the number of weeks out of forty my body allowed Cameron to grow and develop. The second number is ninety. This represents the number of seconds my son was without oxygen and died. Yes, died! God brought him back to us, but those ninety seconds changed his and our lives forever. At fifteen months old, he was diagnosed with Cerebral Palsy due to a lack of oxygen at birth. To this day we continue learning and educating ourselves to better his life with new therapies, yoga, Botox, counseling, and any new technique that will allow him to live better and will challenge him. He is high functioning with his CP to the point that if we don't mention it to others, they rarely figure it out. That boy is my heart, a gift straight from God who breathed life back into his lungs and gave us a chance to raise him, love him, and allow us to experience the gifts he has yet to fully discover. But we see all of it shining through every day. God has great plans for this one.

Forty weeks pregnant? Y'all, that's a laugh! It's so much more. It's the struggle becoming pregnant. The unexpected challenges to remain pregnant. Experiencing the rush of the highs and the heartache of the lows during the journey. That feeling of helplessness as you just can't seem to grasp hold and take control of the spiraling chaos into which you are thrown. It will take time, but you must learn to be gentle with yourself when things don't go according to plan or when you think you have made mistakes and failed. Just because something didn't go as planned doesn't make you a failure. Extend grace to yourself and others, even during your difficult times. Learn to cope with your ever-changing capabilities, restrictions, and disappointments along the way. Let things go, girl! Enjoy the quiet moments because you will cling to them for comfort later.

One thing is for sure, not a single pregnancy of mine lasted forty weeks! However, it was my journey to becoming a mom, and I'm glad they each turned out the way they did.

Andrea Holman

3
Delivery of a Baby Does Not a Mother Make

You may think that some things you have experienced in life were a waste, like I do. Maybe you have spent time beating yourself up over past mistakes, but I'm here to tell you that those moments you hope and pray that no one will ever find out about are exactly what God can use to help you rise! To take you where it is that He needs you to go. To guide you to the purpose He has waiting for you to live out in this lifetime. Nothing is ever wasted if you turn it over to God. He can use everything for His glory, including your difficult, gut-wrenching, and painful moments.

Motherhood for me, if I'm being very honest, was something I had to grow into. It didn't automatically appear within me, like a light switch being turned on to brighten a room, when I delivered our first son. Don't misunderstand me, I loved him dearly, and when I stroked the bottom of his foot while he was laying the NICU room, my heart skipped a beat. But there was something evading me, something I just couldn't place my finger on. It was just out of reach, and each time my outstretched hand attempted to grasp at the feeling, it closed around an emptiness that passed through my fingers. I didn't realize at the time that the feeling I was grasping for was *bonding*. I was struggling; let me share with you why.

We each have our doubts while becoming a mom, our secret issues that plague us during our pursuit of Motherhood, but I experienced something along my journey that I really didn't expect. With the delivery of my son, my body had shut down and robbed me of my right to deliver my baby. I had to have an emergency caesarian section due to many complications. They had to rip him from my body in ninety seconds, from the moment he stopped breathing! Let me tell you, those moments are surreal and forever etched on my heart and mind. After it was all said and done, I was left with feelings of failure, anxiety, and fear, and a straight-up lack of fulfillment from the whole experience. This is when I experienced the unbearable thought that "Delivery of a Baby Does Not a Mother Make!"

Everyone around me assumed I had it all together, and things were going well. And sure, we seemed absolutely happy, and I definitely loved my little guy. He was healthy, the house was clean, and I got up every day with the intention to be the best version of me! However, what they couldn't see was that the weight of my own judgment held me captive. My thoughts, expectations, and disapproval of myself were far worse than anything anyone else could say or do to make me feel inadequate as a mom. I was losing control of my life. Everything changed after the delivery. Yes, many things change after you have kids, but these were things with much deeper meaning. I was unable to recover emotionally at a fast enough pace to cope with all the changes, and my agonizing thoughts continued to grow. God love Luke—no matter how hard he tried, he could not say the right words or do anything to make these go away. It was my internal struggle that I needed to deal with, although I was so grateful for his encouragement and support through it. I thought because I seemed to react differently than other moms that clearly, I was doing something wrong! Adding to the pain was the continued judgment I felt from others, even when it was a figment of my imagination.

After my first epic failure, in my mind, of not being able to deliver my sweet baby on my own, my next episode for judgment came before we even left the hospital! I have a healthy respect for all the medical staff who worked with me prior to my delivery and all those who assisted after, but there was one I referred to as "Scary Nurse," whom I'll never forget! She was the breastfeeding nurse, and I am positive she was very good at her job because she had a lot of knowledge to pass on. But I was so overwhelmed with the swirling of emotions in my heart and mind, along with my body trying to recover, that by the time we got around to talking about my decision of how I would give my child sustenance for life, I was beyond an emotional mess.

My nurse entered the room with an earnest voice, announcing that she was here to counsel me, give me tips, and explain any questions I had about feeding my baby. Now, I don't remember a whole lot about her instructions and the tips for feeding, but at some point during her explanation, my ears started to pay close attention to the words coming out of her mouth. She was talking about the length of time breastfeeding was going to take, each time he was hungry. I really don't know what she said, but this was mostly the gist:

> Scary Nurse: "Now you're going to get the baby and hold it just like a football tucked into your arms..."

> Me, to myself: *Well, everyone knows that...*

> Scary Nurse: "...and then you are going to breastfeed 15 minutes on this side, switch to the other side and feed another 15 minutes, burp him, change the diaper and then put him back to sleep. You will do this every two hours until your baby can start going longer between feedings!"

> Me, possibly audibly: COME AGAIN?

I sat there with a dazed look on my face for a moment, and then I chirped up, because THIS is what I understood her to say: "So, you're going to do this process that will take about 30-45 minutes each time, then he will sleep roughly two hours until he wakes up again. Then, before he wakes up, you have to fall back asleep—which will probably take 10-20 minute—and he is going to wake up within another hour and a half!" I was like, "Nope! Pump the brakes, 'cause this isn't happening!"

Now ladies, it wasn't just my lack of sleep that crept into my mind, it was also the health of my son! I was worried I wouldn't be able to tell how much the baby was getting to eat and if he would be gaining the right amount of weight, and the worry seemed within reason—he was premature, after all!

Not to mention, I really needed my sleep to recover from the emergency C-section! Plus, if I were the one with the food supply, I knew I would be getting up every night until I could store milk for Luke to help! They told me the baby would be fine, that I was just going to monitor his bowel movements as well as his urine output to confirm he was getting enough nutrition! I was thinking, *Who do I look like, the "Poop Whisperer"?* At this point, I was beside myself with doubt thinking I couldn't do it! Plus, in my mind it didn't make sense for me to either! After all, I was still reeling from the unimaginable delivery and near-death experience of my son. I was physically healing and having all these thoughts of guilt that I didn't quite understand. I decided that a formula-fed baby would be just fine.

However, ladies, you know how our emotions can swing back and forth. One moment we are smiling and singing a sweet lullaby to the baby, taking in every inch of their beautiful face to remember how sweet they are, and then suddenly we are ugly crying because we know this won't last. Soon they will be screaming, stomping off up the stairs and slamming their door because they can't stand to hear you even breathe! We have a lot to process emotionally during this season of life. By the time the at-home health nurse came to visit me and check in on our sweet little bundle of joy, I was an irrational, devastated mess over my feeding choice. I felt that I had made the worst decision, and there was no going back! All I had were doubts, tears, and questions to offer her. Would I stunt his growth because he drank formula? Would he be healthy enough? Do I win the award for Most Horrible Mom Ever?! My nurse just smiled sweetly and told me, "Honey, if you want to breastfeed him, you can start today. There is still time." My head cranked around as if I were an owl sitting on my perch in the tree. *WHHAAAAT?* I said to myself. We discussed in depth my options, along with acknowledging that he was thriving and doing well. He had developed jaundice before leaving the hospital, but he was recovering well with at-home light therapy, and he was growing nicely. So physically he was healthy and strong. It was just my emotional state that needed dealing with. After a while of talking, I decided that I had indeed made the right choice for our situation. It was at this point that I was able to find peace within and I was able to move forward past that roadblock in my mind.

Whether or not to breastfeed our babies is an agonizing choice for us moms, and it's also a touchy subject! We lean toward judgment of ourselves and others for this very personal decision and honestly, we should not. What I can tell you is this: You must recognize that all situations, babies, and moms are different, and you need to make the best decision for you and your family. Don't worry about or even listen to judgment from others; just know that "Fed is Best!" and ignore the rest.

I want you to know that while becoming a mother, you will be flooded with many feelings along the way. Some, you very well may not have expected or even be capable of processing on your own. You may be in the middle of this situation currently and thinking to yourself, "I've never heard anyone talk about not bonding with their child right away or being so weighed down with feelings of rejection, failure, or fear, that they could barely function." Just so you know, it does happen, and you are not alone.

I feel there is still a stigma wrapped firmly around these topics of conversation, and that we are encouraged to leave them unspoken, hiding them in the dark. It's hard for us to break into these real conversations, to be brave and push the curtains back to reveal our struggles. We are afraid to be judged and weary of those crazy looks others may toss our way if they have not experienced the same things. We think that shedding light on these feelings could leave us feeling worse, so instead of asking for help, we continue to hide our feelings in the dark.

That's why I want to share some of my experiences with you to help you further understand. Yes, the journey of motherhood is filled with joyful, wonderful, laughable, hilarious moments, but let's get real. There are also moments of feeling lost and isolated, inadequate, and simply *not enough*, all along with being completely overwhelmed! Sometimes, my babies cried so much when I brought them home, I thought for sure there was a baby swap at the hospital. These thoughts are usually fleeting feelings of exhaustion, but sometimes they can find a foothold in your heart and mind causing further doubt.

I remember, after bringing home our first son, when I reached a point where I realized I was encountering a deeper feeling of failure and emptiness inside that needed to be resolved, and I couldn't do it on my own. It was very scary. I had never felt this amount of pressure in my life. How did I know I needed to speak with someone professional? I knew, when these feelings didn't retreat into the edges of my mind and they became the focus of my thoughts, that this wasn't healthy. I needed to speak to someone who was unbiased about my situation. Someone who I could say anything to and maybe they would not think I was crazy or strange. I wanted to cry about my inadequate and unlovable self without being judged because I failed my son and wasn't able to deliver him safely on my own into this world. Worst of all, I wasn't able to control any of it! The birth experience Luke and I had long envisioned was lost, and I was unable to recover who I was supposed to be or how I should feel about who I was becoming, on my own.

My control issues are something I have dealt with since around the age of eight. My need to control everything is a coping mechanism I developed to protect myself. I didn't think it would ever be used to protect myself from the traumatic experience of delivering my own child. Not being able to work through what happened was blocking me from moving forward emotionally or being able to cope with the pressures around me. To even share with you now that I needed help still brings a wave of vulnerability washing over my heart. I mean, no one I knew had ever gone to a therapist, or at least admitted to it! They never talked about issues, failures, or trauma with others. It was to be kept inside, or if you did talk about it, it was kept as a "family matter." Seeking professional help was one of the absolutely hardest things I had ever done in my life up until that point. To this day, I still remember the feeling of walking into her office. I felt fully exposed and unnerved like lying in the dentist chair while he was performing a root canal—without any anesthesia!

I entered the therapist's room, quickly spying a couch in the back of the office. I walked over and pushed myself into the collapsing cushions behind me, trying to disappear. I guess

I thought that if I could just scoot back far enough, maybe I would blend in with the couch and she wouldn't know I was there! Much to my dismay, that did not work. I knew the onslaught of emotions from years of pain that were about to be unleashed, and I didn't want to experience any of them. More than that, I was afraid of what it might truly expose about myself.

My start to therapy was rough. At first, I stonewalled her and would sugarcoat things, again trying to control the narrative and situation. But she was on to me, and she wasn't having any of that. It took us some time to work through the origins of my feelings, my experiences as a child, my control issues, and the brutal birth of my first child. We discussed how the collective trauma of all these things brought me to a place of emotional shutdown, within which I was held back from fully bonding with my son. It was almost like my mind had subconsciously created a barrier to protect me because I had almost lost him during the delivery. Looking back, I can visualize the moment my emotions started to shut down and I can't say I would have been able to stop it. It truly was a defense coping mechanism that, only now, I can identify, and I have been able to change the outcome through hard work and prayer.

There were many layers of emotions, fears, and self-awareness I needed to work through before healing could begin breaking down the defenses I had built. I realized that Luke and

Cameron loved me for who I was, and that was all there was to it. They weren't asking me to be someone I wasn't; they just wanted to experience me for who I was. I was Cameron's mom, and no one was able to fill that role better than me, and God had designed me to accomplish the task. It didn't mean I was going to be perfect at it, but I was who Cameron required. I was so afraid of making more mistakes and continuing to fail him that for a long time I was unable to just lean into the joy of being his mom. God sent this little man to me wrapped in a unique purpose. There was something special he could only retrieve within that relationship with me. I was meant to encourage, prepare, and guide him through the difficult, challenging trials of life so he could rise through the journey.

Which is exactly what has happened. Surviving what happened at the start of his life was a miracle, but his challenges through it have been at times devastating and incredible. My son has been through much in his short life. He has experienced gut-wrenching hardships physically, emotionally, and neurologically. There isn't anything I wouldn't do for him to show him I love him, and I sure have strived to make that a point in his daily life. I have shared with him this special truth his whole life:

> *"There is nothing you could ever do that will take my love from you. I may be disappointed in your decisions and behavior and even become greatly angry with you, but my love is constant and never*

ending. You need to know that you can openly share your good and bad with me. Your secrets you think I won't understand, your deepest concerns about life, and every moment of joy you attain. I will never stop loving you, protecting you, and guiding you."

I have extended a version of this to each of my kids through the years. They can feel it when I say it because it's real and solidified by my actions they encounter.

By reaching out for help through therapy and leaning into prayer, I was able to find peace. At least for temporary bouts of time. It was a good thing, too, because life was about to get very messy! Out of our four kids, three were born prematurely, which also meant they slept through the night, until practically reaching their due dates. This created a false sense of belief in our "Supreme Parenting Skills." We thought we had it all figured out, and we would share our great wisdom with others, trying to help them figure out what they were doing wrong. How arrogant of us! Clearly, there were a lot of things we had forgotten about those baby days! It must have been all the sleep deprivation causing chunks of missing memories, like the smell of vomit and poop on a freshly fed, bathed, and changed baby. Or the nights spent playing the "Whose turn is it to feed the baby this hour?" game. All while trying to look presentable, seem like you have it all together, and take on the world! I found that no matter how good you think you are, you can reach a point where you might just break. It happens to us all. We did know some things, but we were not prepared for the challenges we faced during our parenthood journey together, especially not the kids' diagnoses and the ongoing commitment required to make all the chaos work. I am sure there are a few of you who can understand when I say that I certainly was not winning the "Mom of the Year" award anytime soon! For me it seemed like one failure after the next where mothering was concerned. I had to hold tight to the fact that I knew God was in control of it all, and there was purpose in this seemingly chaotic hot mess called my life!

However, I do want to share with you some of the most comical moments during this journey. Because there is a lot of funny that goes along with becoming a mom, and the laughter is a critical part of what keeps you going!

I started experiencing memory issues after the birth of my first son, and I noticed that it became progressively worse with each baby. I've heard this referred to as "Momnesia." I know it's real because sometimes I can't remember even simple words! My biggest issue is remembering birth dates, and I doubt that any of you have suffered it as epically as me!

By the time our little girl (and fourth kid) Brooklynn was born, I was in full-swing Momnesia mode. There were so many things I couldn't recall. I was always a list keeper, writing things down or using my phone to create a schedule for the ongoing chaos that was my life, but when she came along, I had to take it to another level and include color coding to keep things straight! When you have a husband, four kids, and two fur babies with activities, sports, school, or doctor visits you're in charge of coordinating, there is no other way to go.

When Brooklynn was born, I arrived at the hospital and was admitted on July 23rd. This was the date I remember. Many things become a blur for an expecting mother once she passes through those hospital doors! I was having another cesarean section and mentally trying to prepare myself for what was about to happen. Our girl arrived with ten little fingers and toes, and she was perfect! I must share that I was heavily medicated throughout the entire process, of course, because it was a surgery. The anesthesia doctor had to give me additional medication toward the end of the delivery, as I started having an anxiety attack. Luke thought it was a good idea to show me a picture of just our baby girl's head sticking out of my belly! After seeing that, the weight of the moment settled on me, my brain started to process what my body was really going through, and I started to freak out! I really don't do well with needles, surgery, the operating room, doctors, or basically anything hospital oriented. I'm sure I'm not the only one who doesn't enjoy being poked and prodded.

Plus, I was absolutely exhausted before I even arrived. For a mom with kids, going to the hospital and having three days to actually sleep through the night while essentially being waited on hand and foot was like a dream vacation. I didn't want to go home! Well, I did miss the kids, but I really had been enjoying my rest! However, we were discharged after a few days, and then began the argument over our daughter's date of birth!

Now please remember, I was heavily medicated and unconscious for some of the delivery. After we returned home with our daughter, I realized that I wasn't sure on what date she was actually born. I thought it was July 23rd. Luke and two of my best friends swore on July 25th. One thing was for certain—I, her own Mother, had no idea of her actual birth date! Luke's only jobs were to take pictures and remember when each of our kids were born. I mean, come on! He didn't even have to coach me through pushing! (To his credit, he was instrumental in taking care of and encouraging me through my fears while I was in the hospital. He was an excellent partner through it all… and he took great pictures.)

Well, her date of birth had to be settled. So, off to the safety deposit box I went to grab the baby sign they make for the bassinets, which had her birth date, as well. I was such an emotional mess and committed to proving she was born on the 23rd! It turns out she wasn't. She was born on the 25th! Go figure. No "Mom of the Year" trophy again for me!

On any given day while out running errands, this can be a true struggle for me. The very first time my nemesis appeared was in the form of a sickly-sweet smile peering from behind the pharmacy drive-through window. I felt a pit form in my stomach, and I started to sweat! Oh, she meant well, but as her mouth started to form the seemingly innocent question that escaped her lips, I wanted to sink into a hole. "What's the date of birth?" As if I knew! I looked up with apologetic eyes and replied with a name only, thus beginning an awkward stare-off like something out of a TV sitcom. It became a game of sorts, at least for me, and when they asked me that question I would reply, "Oh, just pick a kid, there's four of them!" The pharmacist would laugh until I said, "No, I'm serious!" There are still days I consider tattooing those dates on my wrist! I blame the kids because they gave me the dang Momnesia, and yes, I am still claiming the lasting effects, even though the youngest is ten!

There were many days I felt scattered and unhinged, like I could just jump right off the pages of my story and erase the moment I was in. I wanted God to pick me up and place me exactly where I was supposed to be. Which in my mind was somewhere in the future part of my story, where things were calm, and I had it all together. It says in the Bible that our lives are like "vapor that appears for a little time and then vanishes away" (James 4:14). I didn't understand why God couldn't just let me blow on over to the right part of my life to live in a more effortless part of my story. But God doesn't operate that way. He distinguishes what we want versus what is necessary for us to withstand each storm we experience, so we can grow. He wants us to thrive! But what is required to build us, sharpen us, and create the awareness that is vital for the next chapter of our story only reveals itself through the storm. There are no short cuts to reach it. We must endure and lean on Him for guidance, knowledge, and discernment. It takes hard work, a willing spirit, and the mindset of a warrior to keep fighting!

I remember telling myself as a young mom so, so, so many times, *You will never measure up.* Maybe you find yourself there now in that very place or you've been there for a long time. Do you know the Bible talks about measuring up and being enough? Yes, it does. I started thinking about the stories I heard as a child and one specifically about a woman who was a wife and a mother, and everyone wanted to be like her. She had it together, and all who lived in the village thought well of her. It's also one of my favorite stories—the Proverbs 31 Woman! Let me tell y'all, she was a Boss!

The story of the Proverbs 31 Woman is a focus for most women studies in the church. I have heard about her my whole life. She is the very depiction of the best mom, wife, homemaker, and all-around woman *ever.* I always compared myself with her, and if I were falling short, then I just knew I must be a failure according to God. The problem was, I fell short every day!

How could I keep up with her? So instead of being encouraged by the story, she became someone I used to beat myself up with over and over again. It irritated me to no end when other women and men would reference her as the utmost example of achievement. That didn't help me feel any better about myself, and truth be told, I wasn't sure how it could make any mom suffering from those similar feelings feel good about herself either. I would smile and nod in agreement but inside, I secretly wished people would forget about her story in the Bible.

In case you aren't familiar or need a refresher, here's the woman I tried to emulate:

> She seeks wool and flax,
> And willingly works with her hands.
> She is like the merchant ships,
> She brings her food from afar.
> She also rises while it is yet night,
> And provides food for her household,
> And a portion for her maidservants.
> She considers a field and buys it;
> From her profits she plants a vineyard.
> She girds herself with strength,
> And strengthens her arms.
> She perceives that her merchandise is good,
> And her lamp does not go out by night.
> She stretches out her hands to the distaff,

And her hand holds the spindle.
She extends her hand to the poor,
Yes, she reaches out her hands to the needy.
She is not afraid of snow for her household,
For all her household is clothed with scarlet.
She makes tapestry for herself;
Her clothing is fine linen and purple.
Her husband is known in the gates,
When he sits among the elders of the land.
She makes linen garments and sells them,
And supplies sashes for the merchants.
Strength and honor are her clothing;
She shall rejoice in time to come.
She opens her mouth with wisdom,
And on her tongue is the law of kindness.
She watches over the ways of her household,
And does not eat the bread of idleness.
Her children rise up and call her blessed;
Her husband also, and he praises her:
"Many daughters have done well,
But you excel them all."
Charm is deceitful and beauty is passing,
But a woman who fears the Lord, she shall be praised.
Give her of the fruit of her hands,
And let her own works praise her in the gates.
(Proverbs 31:13-31)

It wasn't until I stopped to take a deep dive into how to apply her example to my life that I began to grasp the breadth of her story. I wanted to be a Godly mother just like her! To my dismay, focusing on her story, achievements and gifts created way too much pressure. To know that she was operating on that level and still went through countless sleepless nights and cloth diapers; was a wife, a seamstress, and a top chef; all in addition to having a real estate business and being a wine connoisseur and a philanthropist… she was more like the first Superwoman! What did that teach me? That she was beyond my capability to keep up with, and I would never attain her level of success in motherhood!

I mean, who could really deliver all of those things? I began pulling apart her life one piece at a time to find a hidden weakness and to make me feel better about mine. As I pursued with purpose my intentions to pick her apart, my heart only became heavier. Which was unexpected. With each new discovery, I unraveled invaluable nuggets of love, patience, dedication, and a passion to care for others. I realized that I was doing the very thing that I hated when practiced against me: I was judging her! The very woman meant to inspire me, as well as one whom God knew I could learn amazing things from, if I would open my heart and receive it. Let me tell you, that took some work on my end because I was set on being right. Being wrong was too painful to face and meant I may never reach the true path to uncover who I really was! Through much prayer and finally recognizing that I shouldn't compare myself to her but rather seek life with a heart like hers, I was able to appreciate the gift of her story. She was the original "Bible Boss Lady!" for a reason. Her neighbors even thought well of her husband because of her character and how she managed relationships, household, money, business, and interactions with the community. She was content with her life as a mom, wife, friend, and neighbor. Her story exhibits strength and a clear, firm grasp of her own value. She had a fulfilling, successful life in all aspects within the household while pursuing a career. As women, we must stop undervaluing who we are by comparing ourselves to those around us. Just like the Proverbs 31 Woman, with a focused heart for God's path for her, she was able to embrace her authentic self and live fully in who she was. That was her gift, and it's also each of ours for the taking. God wants us to fully recognize who we are and be encouraged by the Proverbs 31 Woman. We should each strive to reach our full potential, but we know in doing so, there is no magic shortcut. It takes commitment, strength, and consistency. Being Mom is by far the most rewarding and exhausting experience of my life. I wouldn't change any portion of it. Only in trusting God through it all is there hope through it.

Everyone parents differently, and this is definitely where our individual gifts help us flourish. It's also where feeling the lack of them creates self doubt and helps us fall short. We all do fall short, though, and God is there to help guide us through as well as supply our strength for the long haul. My life today would be impossible without a relationship with God. Without the struggles and the feelings of pain, fear, doubts and anxiety, I would not be the person I am today either. There is nothing that should ever diminish you from being the person God intends for you to be. It may take time to arrive, but if you stay focused on Him, you will reach the destination and discover your authenticity along the way.

God tells us in the Bible that He will not allow pain without something new being born (Isaiah 66:9). Guess what—after the pain something new *is* born! This applies to you, too, and that's exciting! Becoming a mom is a full journey from the beginning to the end, and I'm not talking about the delivery. There is hardship in carrying a child and crazy pain in the delivery of a child. But what we learn from it changes us as it leaves emotional, physical, and spiritual marks across our life. This journey is new, our focus is new, and we are driven with new purpose. This new little baby's life is solely dependent on you! So, what do you do if you feel as though you don't measure up? This is the secret gift I offer you: Focus your heart of God, and "Be You, 'Cause I'm Taken!"

Through my journey of becoming a mom, I learned to create coping mechanisms that worked best for me. I must say that not all coping mechanisms are created equal, and some are not even safe. I can only tell you that for every mom with whom I have discussed raising children, this practice was an unmistakable part of their survival techniques, whether they realized it or not. Some of my favorite strategies are prayer, laughter, hanging with my friends, therapy, anxiety medicine, and puppies. That's right, I said it! I bought two puppies to help me cope through many of my anxieties. I'm not ashamed of it! Although my husband about lost his ever-loving mind with the most recent puppy purchase. She is taking way too long to potty train, and he keeps looking at her like she's on a very short deadline for achieving this task! I think she'll make it. I see him passing her extra treats when he doesn't think I'm watching.

Everyone's coping mechanisms are different, and you should use what works best for you. Why? Because not every mom is wired the same. We have similar experiences, emotions, and—if we are being honest—mom meltdowns. However, our bodies, brains, and emotions react and process differently. Some coping styles you can identify right away. Like the physical activity copers—the walkers, runners, and tennis players who use any activity to keep moving so they can stay grounded. There are the social copers, who make play dates, create mom groups, and volunteer for all the school activities. Then you have the Girls Night Out copers. These are the story tellers, the wine sippers, and the "hang out 'til midnight in their slippers" girls!

Some coping skills we come to lean on, however, are kept shrouded in darkness. These habits may have started out innocently, yet somewhere along the way we accidentally indulged more heavily or may have pressed harder into them for comfort, giving them the opportunity to claim a foothold in our lives. All of which is something we never expected or wanted. I'm so thankful I was able to journey through these chapters in my story without leaning on those coping mechanisms. I have heard stories that have made my heart ache for these sweet ladies. It's a vulnerable story shared by many that entangle our hearts through direct experience or compassion. For those who find themselves in that moment, know that this is not permanent, it's just a season, and you can prevail if you will steel yourself against the agony required to reach the other side.

It's a cruel twist in your story when you have reached such a vulnerable place in which you feel broken. For myself, asking for help and knowing that I was beyond my own capability to heal was the hardest thing I ever did. I was seeking a peace which eluded me, and which I felt belonged to someone else for many years. In order to find my peace, I had to turn it over to God. My family needed me not just to be present, but to thrive and be healthy. It was an unattainable goal while I held onto the fear, control, and anxiety so tightly. I had to retrain my thoughts and learn to focus on the positives in my life, express my emotions by writing, start speaking self-affirmations, praying, exercising, therapy, and utilizing medicine. Each of which played a significant role in my healing. It took a lot of deep searching within my heart and mind. Traveling to places within that were long sealed and locked away. I had to realize that God was with me through each moment when I suffered, bled, or felt lost. I was in His protection, grace, and mercy through it all, and I was never lost to Him.

If you have experienced a situation like this, are headed in this direction, or are currently right in the middle of it, I invite you to be gentle with yourself. This is a long journey and I know you don't want to hear that, but your emotions and spirit can be wounded easily during these moments. I want to encourage you to please not feel ashamed of where you find yourself or offer harsh judgment either. I promise that you are not alone in the struggle of seeking deliverance from something that has grasped ahold of you and is unwilling to relinquish control without a fight! But you have a place to lean into that will give you the power to prevail. You must find this new place to lean into because the old ways have hindered your path to this fight. Open your heart and allow God to be your focus, your center. He will become your strength. His peace will cover your life and create a new beginning within your heart. He has always been there waiting for you to reach out for Him.

I'm not sure if one ever fully becomes delivered as a mother. What I mean is that motherhood is an ever-changing rhythm of life we move within, and there are new steps to learn almost every day as we navigate the challenges and feelings we face. It would be boring if we knew everything about being a mom from the beginning. There would be no mystery left to the job or comprehensive discoveries to be made! What's the fun in that? We actually may have decided to not have kids if we knew all the heartache we would suffer from a seemingly innocent bundle of joy (or the number of diaper blowouts coming our way). No matter what you do, you can never protect yourself or your kid from life's heartbreaks and pain. Each time they suffer, so do you. It's part of being a mom, and sometimes it becomes a heavy price to pay, one that we can hardly bear.

The secret of it all is what's so amazing! Who knew you could be so deprived of sleep, covered in puke, and—let's face it—poop, and still have your heart melt when they flash a little smile because they passed gas? They are so stealthy while squirming their way into your heart! It took years of sweet little pats, kissing boo-boos, and learning the rhythm of each kid to achieve that next level of motherhood! I feel like there are many stages I have passed through, but I'm still in a never-ending, maturing cycle. I'm not sure when one fully becomes delivered as a mother, but I'm glad there is still a shroud of mystery in the becoming. There are things that still need to be unraveled with each new experience of becoming a mom!

I realize, looking back, that I was routinely transforming into a mom, and that I was exactly where I needed to be each time in the storm to expose the lessons I required for life. I was left feeling exposed when the storms howled and riddled devastation through my life. The storms were required so I could learn to withstand the rage it threw against me, whether it was from my own doing or other circumstances. It would take those storms to teach me that I was able to find sure footing in new rhythms that arose and to stand on solid ground with God guiding me through it. Only by leaning on Him in the storm was I able to break through the fear to reach the other side, emerging stronger, more capable, and more authentic. Only God can pick up the pieces in your life and create something new from its pain.

Finding my way back to God was never knowingly hard. I knew where He was the whole time. He was a whisper, thought, a prayer away. In my mind and heart, I knew what was necessary. However, my stubbornness and control issues blocked my heart from responding and fully embracing myself! For years I believed that God wanted to change me, but He didn't. However, I learned that He always knew who I was, and He wanted more than anything for me to accept myself. Learning this allowed me to be more open to His voice and to more easily release control to God, so I was able to focus on becoming a mom.

4
I Quit the Family!

God has granted Luke and me the wonderful gift of becoming parents. Parenthood for us, probably like all of you, is a never-ending cycle of learning how to accomplish new skills and techniques to conquer what your kids throw at you! I have never personally met a perfect parent. Have you? Some days, you are just trying to survive, and other days you're like, "I've got this whole parenting thing totally figured out!" Did you know that in order to raise kids, you can't just rely on your own parenting skills? I didn't! You need degrees from the "School of Hard Knocks," too. That's right. They consist of, but are not limited to, degrees in education, special education, psychology, religion, human resources, human development, fashion design, cosmetology, biology, anatomy, sex education, family studies, cultural studies, public health, culinary skills, and a doctorate degree! Who knew? And this just takes you through the sixth grade!

The first two boys we were blessed with were what people refer to as "typical boys." They would scream, roughhouse, wrestle with Daddy, and hug Momma, all while pretty much following the house rules. Of course, they had their crazy moments, but nothing ever outlandish.

Our first son, Cameron, never gave us any trouble. Being the first child, we poured all our parenting knowledge into him, so he received the most, and we expected the most from him. Because with all our combined knowledge, he should just know better. Right? I remember the first time he ever talked back to me. I was standing in the kitchen, and he was about twelve years old. I stopped dead in my tracks, turned on my heels to face him and said, "Have you lost your mind? I don't know who this child is, but you better go up to your room until you find the boy I raised. Then you can come back down and apologize." He actually did it, too! He never challenged us in our parenting management style. He made me feel like an excellent mom as far as his behavior and obedience!

Our second son, Ethan, was a little more challenging . . . and a biter. I mean, you needed to make sure flesh was still attached to the bone if he got ahold of you! As we were challenged with his behavior and started seeking solutions, we discovered he was dealing with sensory and impulsivity issues. We spent years working to help him find his rhythm in this world, and we established a strong rhythm for our family. In each season of our parenting, there were new, surprising challenges and chaos endured. Learning how to accommodate each of our kids' needs forced us to be more flexible, master new skills, change tactics, and create scheduling techniques to manage with just the two boys. We danced along to the beat and were lulled into a serious false sense of "Parenting Mastery," which would soon be put to the test!

While raising our third son, Austin, we started to feel a mysterious rhythm, and the steps eluded us no matter how we moved. We couldn't seem to keep our steps in sync and often seemed to fall over each other's feet! Austin was the most spirited, high-energy child I had encountered to that point in my life, and yet there was a sense of familiarity in his chaos. Even as an experienced mom, I was positive I would not survive the out-of-sync beats of his cadence! They were fast, unorthodox, innovative, and layered with complexity all at the same time. It drove me crazy that I wasn't able to grasp his tempo. However, we were given the gift of raising him. So even if it killed us, we were going to learn this new dance! We knew we were not always going to be in sync, but all the beats still made music, right?

I'll never forget the time we were at a local kids' inflatable facility, hanging out while the kids played, when our evening was interrupted with screams and blood. We had been there most of the evening, eating pizza and listening to the music pumping through the speakers while watching our kids run through the maze of fun. Luke and I sat toward the front of the room, so we had a good view of the full arena when all of a sudden, I heard my name being yelled from across the facility. Not over the speakers, mind you, but from a worker, who was a friend of ours. He was yelling in a very specific, highly concerned, and scared voice. You know, the one that makes the hair on the back of your neck stand up and goose bumps creep down your arms? As I turned to acquire the yelling target, I could see in the distance someone running toward us holding a kid pushed straight up in the air, above their head. It only took a hot second to recognize that it was Austin he was holding and just one second longer to fixate on the blood streaming down his shirt and pants and all over the worker's face! Thank God we knew the young man, and he had known Austin since he was a baby, or he would have been completely freaked out from all the blood! As he drew closer, he all but tossed him into my arms as I reached toward him. We immediately ran into the bathroom to clean him up, and an off-duty nurse who happened to be there peeked in to take a look at the damage. She said, "Yep, that's absolutely going to need stitches." So, over the river and through the woods, to the emergency room we go! We took off!

The full story began to unfold in the bathroom as we were cleaning Austin's face. Our friend had seen Austin on the inflatable and really didn't think much of it as he was big enough to make it through, and he was familiar with the rides in the facility. A few moments later, he heard kids screaming, so he turned to investigate. As he followed their pointing fingers, he saw our other two sons' horrified faces looking down to the concrete floor between the inflatables. He took off, knowing someone had fallen! He scaled over the side and jumped down onto the floor, where he found Austin lying with his chin gashed open. He picked him up, jumped back up over the inflatable, and came running. I still remember thinking at this point, "Thank God he had been training to join the military, or he may not have been able to clear the jumps required to reach him and pull him to safety!" Austin was all muscle and a very solid kiddo. Not just anyone could have pulled him out of there. God certainly places us in the right place and at the right time. There is no doubt about that.

Piece by piece, I was able to extract more information from our sons, and they explained that Austin was upset because they were racing through the inflatable, and he wasn't able to beat them to the end. So he, of course, did what any reasonable little brother would do in this predicament . . . he climbed over the edge and scrambled down the side to where he could jump across the maze, landing in perfect time to win the race! That was his plan; however, when he jumped, he didn't clear the gap. So, to my older sons' horror, all they could do was watch as he bounced off the other side, landing on the concrete below after hurling his body through the air. To this day, we still tell this epic story, and Austin continues to push all the limits with his competitive nature.

While we were at the urgent care facility that evening with him, the doctor was stitching up his chin—which he was sticking out proudly—and I told the nurses, "Take a good look at him, ladies, because he will be back!" They just started laughing, and I wondered how many times I would have to live through this. The funny thing is, we never returned with him to that urgent care facility. By the time he was injured later in life, we required a much more advanced hospital!

Back at the inflatable facility, Austin had been competing with his older brothers. Does that ring a bell of familiarity for you? For him, the only sensible course of action in that moment was to execute a short cut and win! However, what he didn't yet know is that often those shortcuts come with more risks and snares along the way that we don't recognize and certainly can't see coming. Most of the time, in order to gain knowledge from the lesson, it takes the full measure of its course to acquire its effect. Such are the stories we have of raising our fly-by-the-seat-of-his-pants third son, Austin. Even the infamous fire alarm pull at daycare when he was three years old didn't compare to this fiasco! With that incident, he was able to meet the firemen and climb into their big red truck! It wasn't much of a deterrent for him to never pull the alarm again, although he didn't. I couldn't even be mad at him for the incident because I came to the conclusion that he was helping the daycare operate within proper county codes, as they didn't have a cover plate over the handle. You better bet they put a case over it the next day after Austin blatantly made them aware of their violation! I guess some things you can learn quickly and never forget. Especially when there is a high cost or trauma involved.

Austin seemed to literally do anything that popped into his head, and his mouth was no better! He has what we call a "Zero-Filter Capacity." That reminded me of someone else I knew as well... me! Oh, the phone calls we have received about our baby boy over the years! You know those families you would see with crazy kids, and the mom and dad look like they've lost their minds? For the first two years of raising Austin, that was pretty much us in a nutshell. We literally had a twenty-minute window to complete any task in public until his inability to cope wore off, and a scene would ensue. We were held captive for the first two years of his life. We would leave work, pick up kids, complete the kids' therapies, eat dinner, conduct baths, and go to bed, just to get up the next day and start all over again. Austin required a strict schedule, venting moments, quiet moments, and constant food; everything for our family was determined around his constrained needs. I was painfully aware of the effect it was having on our family, and at the same time, I felt inadequate to approach any change.

I compare the early years of learning how to parent Austin as trying to learn one of the most difficult ballet techniques: dancing *en pointe*. This is when a dancer places all her body weight on the tip of one foot, using a special shoe, to strike the perfect pose. Although I certainly did not perform it with that much grace, I tried my hardest over and over to strike and hold that perfect pose while parenting him! Swaying with him on the dance floor was a delicate and will-bending act amidst the "eggshells" of tolerance. We were jumping his combative kicks and jiving to his wild tantrum rhythms. I watched his body language for levels of agitation and focused on his eyes to examine the level of excitement he was exuding. This helped me detect max capacity and reach him before his coping capability hit overload!

I remember once we were at a school play for Ethan, which was one of the few events we would venture out to with Austin because he could run around in the back of the gym behind all the seats if needed. After the play, all the kids went to dance on the stage, and the excitement level in the room went up a notch. We were heading to a local ice cream shop to celebrate, and right before we left, I caught a glimpse of Austin's face from across the room. I promise you, he had a smile stretching the entire length of his face and he looked just like the Cheshire Cat from *Alice in Wonderland*! I knew I was pushing my luck taking him out. However, this was a celebration for Ethan, and we wanted to create special memories for him with his friends. We went for ice cream and chatted with our friends while the kids hung out in the store. Austin ate his ice cream and was doing fine, and I felt a sense of calm settle that I hadn't felt in a long while. I lowered my guard and started to engage in conversation, and that's when it happened. He ran straight out the front door, right for the street! I almost had a heart attack, and we couldn't move fast enough to reach him because of the position of the tables! Thank God one of our friends, who is a doctor, had just walked outside with her son and caught Austin by the back of his shirt as he went whizzing by, yanking him hard enough to keep him out of the street!

When we arrived home, my body went into a full-blown panic attack. It was the worst attack I had experienced at that point! I was barely able to make it to the top of our stairs, and as I entered my bedroom, I hit my knees sobbing as I attempted to crawl to the bed. Luke was furious with Austin for putting himself in danger and for triggering my panic attack. I was so upset and grieved in my heart for him, because I could see the pain in his little eyes. I thought for sure this episode would scar him emotionally for life! I had so badly wanted to have a nice evening out for Ethan. To watch him perform and celebrate him without any outburst, breakdowns, or dangerous situations arising. The night had just spiraled into complete chaos.

I started having more panic attacks when Austin turned seven. I believe the combination of my own stress, raising three kids, and holding down two full-time jobs inside and outside of the home, all while trying to maintain a sense of normalcy dealing with our kids' multiple medical diagnoses and doing my part for a healthy marriage put me over the edge just a bit. These stresses, along with the pressure of constantly being on guard for Austin's safety, created a heavy strain on the family. We never had a moment to relax unless he was asleep. He woke up in the morning like lightening, and he could get into dangerous trouble faster than a snake strike! My level of anxiety rose with each passing year, and for me, medication became part of my daily reality and necessary functionality for my blood pressure and anxiety. It was really the next step for me after calming techniques stopped working. Besides, Luke and I were already running kids to the doctors, therapies, and school activities; and as every parent knows, there is no time for panic attacks in a mom's life.

Remember that extreme dance technique I shared earlier? Ballet moves are so precise and complex, they take years to master, and even the greatest dancers find them difficult to execute properly. With Austin, everything about his rhythm seemed to bring disruption, disconnection, and complexity. We didn't expect him to be like our other kids; however, we did expect him to be manageable. It made me crazy because each move was offbeat for me, and I'm a pretty good dancer! My problem was I was striving to master his rhythms. I wanted him to dance and behave within the approved choreographed moves we had established for our family. I should have realized earlier that he was designed with the unique gift to expand and thrust the edges of our dance floor forward so new, lively rhythms could emerge! The more we tried to contain him, the more separated, lost, and out of sync with us he felt. I wish I would have recognized his gift more swiftly and created a space for him to be fierce in his own way, just as I have been allowed to my whole life. However, as "good moms," society scolds us for not having control of our kids' behavior. We're told that we are supposed to raise them properly according to society's expectations and make them learn to follow along in an orderly fashion! What happens when you have "That Child" who breaks all the rules, ignores the boundaries, and seems to do everything within their power to complicate your life?

Well, for me, I almost lost my ever-loving mind! He was a mini-me, and I just knew I wasn't going to be able to reign this one in! He knew where all my buttons were, and he liked to push them and jump up and down to make sure they stayed pushed in! Words like "exasperated" or "devastated" don't begin to cover how I felt with his behavior and for my failed capability to clearly display a level of ability to parent him. It's numbing to have daily reminders of your incompetence and to look in the mirror knowing you'll never measure up to becoming the great mom you envisioned for so long.

Outside of the ongoing struggles we faced with his behavior, that boy had a heart of gold! He was such a giver. Little did we know, he was getting ready to give us so much more than what we could handle. I know people say God will never give you more than you can handle, but *Wow*! All of our alternative moves and radical beats which previously pacified the ever-awaiting erupting storms in our lives were not going to keep up, and we already knew there was a "Strict No-Return Policy" on this kid! I'm joking. Come on, I'm joking! However, we did always say that we must have left the instruction manual for him at the hospital! Austin was beyond a handful. He was loud and stubborn and would change on a dime, like a sensitive and impulsive tornado. This, coupled with the fact that he was so much like ME—I knew we were in way over our heads.

Do you remember when your kids were young, and you would read them bedtime stories? You watched with delight as your child's eyes lit up anticipating what would happen next in the story. However, sometimes the character will have a surprise encounter, go on a wild goose chase or, even worse, take a wrong turn into a deep, dark forest! As the words of our story were falling on the page, I would have given anything to be the one in control of the plot. To be allowed to create memories with less pain, to erase lines in the scenes that flashed through my mind to this day, to create a rosier portrait of our family's story. I would have written a more straightforward outcome with a much less complicated, plot-twisting story line. In doing so, I would have deprived us of the remarkable journey full of twists and turns through mystery, danger, adventure, and enemy attacks on our family. We would have missed our story, and as chaotic as it was, it was still ours.

But how could I have not seen what was happening to my family, you may ask? Well, that's easy. I was living in the middle of it! I have never met any parents who were gifted with a complete awareness of the lessons they were learning from life experiences as they were living through them. It's always easier to look at someone else's situation and recognize what they need to do to fix their mess. I mean, when others share their story with me, and they often do because most everyone I meet spills the beans, I can clearly see what steps need to happen in order to improve their storyline. I can devise an action plan with step-by-step directions, a list of Bible verses, and complete diagrams, plus add an index and include a list of outreach resources for them by the end of our conversation. But my mess? It had hazy surroundings, crushing noises, and the weight of my own judgment holding back any hope of a new story line. What were we missing?

My husband and I have endured our fair share of struggles, just like everyone else. During our extremely difficult times, we resolved to a tactic most people unknowingly utilize to survive their chaos. We compartmentalized our lives into sections. This enabled us to cope with the responsibilities of parenthood, our careers, and others' expectations of us. Along with this, I had to compartmentalize my emotions. If I had uttered the restrained words of fear, stress, and anxiety I had buried into existence, it may have broken us down completely. However, unvoiced or not, this was my reality. It's where I found myself pondering in the dark when the quiet fell over our chaos. I've never been good with silence. It's an uncomfortable space for me, like wearing a wool sweater and not being able to scratch the itch when it rubs against your neck. I had control issues, yes, but I hated the silence even more. Therefore, chaos became my awaiting escape. It was difficult, but I could deal with it. Because allowing the words and thoughts that stalked my mind to spring forth into life, onto the pages of our story, was an entirely different issue all together. Uttering those words meant they were real and not locked behind the layers of safety I had devised. Once uttered, they were able to roam and corrupt our story.

I was in uncharted territory, and I didn't have time to give birth to my emotional baby! For that matter, I didn't have time to take care of it either. Luke and I had to remain focused on the moment and stay on course. We knew if we had made it this far, we could keep going, even in our tattered physical and emotional state. We would rest later! We knew there had to be a more calming place on the other side of this crazy. If we quit now, we would never reach it, and Dear Lord, we had been through too much to give up.

We had suspected for a long while that Austin was struggling with ADHD. With the way he reacted to certain situations, along with his increasing tantrums and anger outbursts, we knew we were dealing with more than just a behavioral concern. There was something going on that he needed more help with than we could give him. We were struggling with obtaining an official diagnosis. Partly, because I felt like a horrible mom for not being able to provide him with what he needed, and partly, because we didn't want him labeled as "That Kid" or "The Problem Child!"

Mommas, you know what I'm talking about! I didn't want him to be treated differently by teachers and kids, though deep inside I had the sickening feeling that he would be, either way. It was the same feeling I had in the pit of my gut when Cameron was diagnosed with CP. I spent hours on the computer doing research. I read about different calming techniques, transitioning processes, and anything else I could find that would help us create a routine for him. The one thing we were sure of was that he needed lots of jumping and playing in his routine to help combat his outbursts. I even gave him warnings before transitioning from one activity to another. We walked on eggshells for six years, just waiting for the hammer to drop in the form of an extreme outburst (and it inevitably did, no matter what we tried)! We knew we could not provide all he needed, we were exhausted, and we were not sure how much longer we could hang on.

When I had my "I Quit the Family" moment, we were way down the path of running in survival mode! We were stretched thin on patience, sleep, and everything in between. Even with that, I never thought that we would end up where we found ourselves that day. I mean, we knew it was becoming increasingly difficult for him to manage his outbursts while maintaining focus in school, but how could we have known what was waiting to unfold as we turned that day's page? We ran straight into a plot twist no one could have seen coming! Unbeknownst to us, Austin would create the perfect moment to utter an infamous statement, one that will live on forever and become the cornerstone for how our family dynamics would be transformed.

The mornings were kept contained with what had become our normal chaotic routines. The kids woke up, hopefully in good moods, and the morning would turn into a blur to rush them out the door! At this point in our lives, we were just trying to contain the chaos, get the kids to the bus on time with backpacks and lunches, and get ourselves out the door to work. There was an exhausting list of tasks we followed each day just to accomplish the morning routine. We both had careers outside the home, but we were fortunate that Luke worked close by and was able to help tag-team the mornings, as well as run to the school quickly if a need arose. Our first two boys were fairly cooperative, but when our third arrived, we no longer had "man-to-man" coverage. We had to switch to "zone defense" in our playbook because we were just outnumbered!

That fateful day had started out like any other. In the afternoon I met the kids at the school bus like normal, and we began our walk home. Mind you, everything was fine. The day was pleasant, the birds were chirping, and we were all smiles and in good moods as the kids chatted with friends. We said our goodbyes to them at the end of the driveway, and the kids took off running into the house, with me bringing up the rear of our troop. Austin came inside and was standing in the kitchen with his back to me. I passed him as I laid my things on the kitchen counter, not really thinking anything of him standing there. I am not sure what the topic of the conversation was, but I know that it turned loud, very quickly. The loud conversation became an argument, and then we were in a deafening shouting match!

Now, I know I am supposed to be the adult in this situation, have control, and be able to manage this tantrum he was having; but honest to God, I just didn't *want to* anymore! I was done having arguments with him that had no rhyme or reason! I was on the ropes and ready for the fight this time. I could not comprehend why he was so belligerent toward me, when I had given so much and had worked so hard to accommodate every need he had for the past six years around all the needs of everyone else in our family. In that moment, I reached my maximum capacity for coping, and it was on.

When I think back on it, I recall the scene in the way I remember watching my brother's boxing matches. Austin and I were exchanging verbal blows, and as our screaming match continued, we both grew angrier. With each sentence we threw across the ring, the decibel factor of our voices grew louder, too. His little face was turning red as the veins in his neck started to bulge, and I was in no better shape, y'all! I suffered from high blood pressure, anxiety, and stress. As he took another swing at my clearly incompetent parenting style, my heart sank with each hit. I knew my face was turning red because I could feel my flushed cheeks! My heart was beating so fast I couldn't hear my own thoughts. My breathing had quickened, and I was sure my left eye was twitching to the Survivor song "Eye of the Tiger" with each word that flew!

The whole argument was ridiculous and over almost as soon as it started! I mean, he was totally fine just minutes prior. He was good all day for his teachers, which I knew because I had not received a phone call. I knew he'd been good for the bus driver on the way home because there was no raised eyebrow at me when he jumped off the bus. He had even acted just fine with all his friends, siblings, and me as we had slowly walked toward the house. But, as soon as we breached the entry way into our home, a different child all together appeared, and he was in a full nuclear meltdown!

At the peak of the argument, he articulated his full displeasure with us. He was so mad that I couldn't grasp what he was trying to express in that moment that he had finally reached his limit of participation with me and our family. He clenched his fists, stomped his foot dramatically on the kitchen floor, and spewed out, "I quit the family!" Without hesitation, my reply formed in my mind and came right out of my mouth challenging his ultimatum. I yelled, "Oh, no! Nobody quits the family before Momma, and Momma ain't quittin'!"

Austin's mouth snapped shut, and his eyes grew wide in a blank stare. Neither of us blinked! After a few moments, I sent him to his room as we both pondered what had taken place—we were both in shock. I think it's one of the few times he actually held his tongue!

Our words hung heavy in the air, and believe me, there was a lot of hot air for them to settle on. Where did my outburst come from? How did I have that comeback ready so fast? I didn't even know why I felt the need to say it. Of course, I wasn't even thinking about quitting the family! Why would I have said that? It was like another mom showed up within me and bared her ugly, truthful soul! You know, that mom we lock away deep down inside under all the red ink; the one with her feelings, broken heart, and fear of what the future held for each of her babies; the one always worried whether she was worthy or good enough for her family? Yeah, *that* mom! Where had she been all this time? She was also strong, amazing, and secure in who she was. We needed her. Most of all, I needed her.

I'm so thankful for Austin's argument and that "I Quit the Family" moment of reckoning. I know some of you may think, "Say what?" and that I'm just horrible! Well, back off, ladies! That's right. I said, *Back Off*! I have such gratitude for the moment we shared. I'm so very glad I didn't recognize his need, because it was then, in one of the lowest, darkest moments that the epiphany was revealed, and I realized our family's binding to our story was unraveling. This is something you would usually want the editor to rewrite or manipulate in the story so the shocking reality of it is easier on your senses, but this moment marked a turning point in our story. This moment provided the opportunity for transformation and for hope.

To my shock, I realized that I was living in what I now call the Quit! Deep inside, I knew it. I could feel it. How could I not? We were six years into this battle with bursts of anger that could challenge even the volcanic eruptions of Mount Kilimanjaro! It just took an unplanned, against-the-ropes, word-swinging fight to expose it and give light to what I already knew. What I had been fighting to hide from everyone, including myself. I am not even sure when it occurred, but somewhere in those years of moving through the motions and trying to survive, I had quit. Not on purpose, mind you. I had stayed where I was comfortable, within the chaos. But this time, I had dived too deep into the pages of my past. I was trying to resolve emotional chapters of hard moments, painful discoveries, exposure of limitations, unmet expectations, and the crushed dreams we had for our kids. And in doing so, I had unknowingly removed myself from being present in the moments with my kiddos. The moments that keep us moms going when everything around us is falling apart . . . those precious moments were lost to me as if written with invisible ink across the pages of my soul. I hoped it wasn't too late to reclaim some of what was lost, to create the story I knew was possible for our family, but there was work to be done and breakthroughs to be had.

Each kid is designed with special gifts and talents that as parents, we are called to encourage, guide, develop, and grow. Austin has incredible talents and the biggest heart for loving others you can imagine. His smile lights up a room, and his hyper spirit is contagious! Others are drawn to his infectious personality, his easy laugh, and his sense of humor. But when he's frustrated and exhausted, you better get ready for a plot twist and hang on tight for the ride, because a shift in the story will soon emerge!

After Austin's attempt to quit the family, we had decided to reach out to our doctor for an evaluation to request treatment for what we suspected he was dealing with. The day of his diagnosis, we were not looking forward to the hard discussions with the doctor. I was already on edge, and Austin gave me no mercy with his behavior as we wrestled him to settle into the tiny room. As we sat squirming uncomfortably in the plastic chairs, and the exam table's paper crinkled beneath Austin rolling around, I could feel the walls start closing in around me. My chest began to tighten, and my anxiety was climbing with each passing minute and crinkle of the paper. He was in a very hyper mood, and no sooner had he jumped onto the exam table than he started swinging his legs and fell onto the floor with a loud thump! I jumped out of my chair and yelled, "Austin! Oh my God, are you okay?" The doctor heard it from outside of the room and swung open the door just in time to see us picking him up off the floor. After she checked on him, we moved straight into delivering our concerns to her, reviewing test results, asking questions, and discussing medication options.

I can't tell you that I took any pleasure in having him diagnosed with what I already knew. It was like a knife pricking at my heart as she breathed life into the words that would describe his behavior. "Mr. and Mrs. Holman, your son has ADHD." I was thinking, *Tell me something I don't know*. It's a diagnosis with which we never wanted him labeled, nor did we want him to endure the struggle throughout his life, yet here we were. We were definitely at the breaking point and professional direction in determining what was the next best move for him was mandatory.

With tears rolling down my face, I told the doctor, "We've done everything we know to do and then some. We've tried schedules, the ten-minute warnings for transitions and calming music to help soothe him during his outbursts. You have to do something else with him, because I'm medicated and I can't take any more!" The doctor explained to us that there was nothing we could have done to prevent him from having ADHD. Nor was there anything we did to cause it. However, in the back of my mind I couldn't help but think that we had passed this down in our genes to him and so, technically, it *was* our fault!

The day of the argument, Austin was spent. Looking back, I really believe he couldn't wait to step foot into his safe place: with me, at home. It's usually where the kids feel the safest and where they are with the ones who love them the most, where they can release frustrations built up from the day. His day was full of pressure, anxiety, and the stress of trying to hold it all together and "fit in." Making it through the day with the added distractions, noise, and complexities of how his mind processes data had to be overwhelming. He needed to express what he was suffering through, and he needed me to support and listen to him, even when I felt like I was failing. He was seeking exactly what I was: someone to recognize that he was giving his very best, but he was drowning, suffering, and ready to quit! Austin and I both had feelings of inadequacy. We were both experiencing the spillover of emotions from the chaos we were in, and we each had our own way of dealing with it.

I was a crippling, emotional mess on the inside while holding close the chapters of my life that were too painful and, frankly, would take too long to resolve! Hiding between the lines of each story was the only way for me to cope. Austin was unable to hide his level of emotions, and his outbursts allowed him to release his pain. His struggles with control were similar to mine, though he was (and still is) even more stubborn, if you can believe that! Both of our routines worked for us. They just didn't work when running at the same time, and they certainly didn't work well overall for the rest of the family. Our reactions and thinking were eerily alike—we just couldn't seem to find a rhythm to move to together. What a pair we made! Was I this difficult to get along with? My friends never complained, at least not to my face… I was starting to think that they were too afraid to.

It turns out, parenting a younger version of myself was more testing than I could have ever imagined. All I know is that my mom, dad, and the Good Lord had some serious patience when it came to dealing with me! Austin's and my coping techniques spilled over onto the pages of our story, splashing blots of ink across moments lost to legend. But their impacts were felt through the ever-changing family dynamics, altering relationships forever. Feeling like I wasn't in control was a devastating blow to my ego. With children, there isn't a full-chapter instructional book you can read to fully prepare yourself for the specific parenting assignment you are granted. Even if there were, and you read it front to back, you are never fully prepared for it! How could you be?

We all get a little lost on the journey while learning how to become parents. We apply our ideas and hold our breath waiting for the outcome of victory or defeat! Even with all the resources at our fingertips, each child has their way of narrating life and devising new concepts to shape life to their needs. As parents, we are left to figure out each kid along the way, and sometimes this creates troublesome chapters we want to weed out of our personal library! And sometimes, this creates a literary masterpiece so uniquely incredible, we are just grateful to be part of it. However, it's when you realize that all those stories in the purged chapters can't be separated from the masterpiece, or you lose the true beauty within the pages that you find the authenticity of your life.

Navigating uncharted waters while parenting is normal. No one has it all figured out. Challenges allow us to expand our capabilities and prepare for battles ahead. Continuing to focus and stay the path brings us closer to the lessons we need in order to reach the other side, and we all want to reach the other side! Right? Even when Luke and I were worn down, tattered physically and emotionally, we knew there was meaning on the edge of our precipice. It wasn't within view, but we were aware of its presence. There are moments etched so deeply in ink across my heart I wish they would disappear, but no amount of scrubbing could remove the stain of their pain. In a twist of irony, the emotions from their moments became a familiar map through which I recall what was not only survived but conquered in order for growth to emerge. The lessons are tied to these emotions with purpose.

Oh, how all the challenges, plot twists, dark blots, and mountaintop treks form the manuscript for an amazing journey of discovering you! When you're living in the "Quit," and I believe everyone does at some point, I hope you realize you are not alone. You may be overwhelmed, trying to close unresolved chapters of your story and finding yourself editing the pages, or you may even find that the quiet elusive chapter you seek is so very far away. Maybe you are where I found myself, unable to find the last bookmark I'd placed, smearing the pages with drying ink, and unable to hear the faint whisper of God because of drowning emotional pain. I had been trying to control the narrative for so long that I was exhausted and unable to just participate in the growing storylines of who we were as a family. I had to come to terms with the fact that I was never meant to be the author. I was a main character in the ongoing chronicles of our life together and what we would become, and that was epic in itself!

My gift was remembering that even though I felt completely cocooned in the chaos, I was never alone. Luke, our kids, and I were all walking in the same story, but experiencing it from different stages within. No matter who is walking by your side, there are parts of your pages always hidden to them. Moments you dare not let others see. Thoughts you dare not let others know. But God always sees and always knows... I needed to remember to whisper Him back into my story. He had been with me through each dark moment, as well as the brightest! Allowing Him to guide me on the journey created a new chapter and revealed a unique, solid beat to steady our steps as we moved.

It was Austin's "I Quit the Family" moment that changed it all! That moment created the gift that would help solidify our story together, spur us on in our resolve, expand our comfort zone beyond its borders, and create a moment that brought God back as the author in the pages of our life! I had lost my way because I wasn't leaning on the One who knew me best, who could comfort me and guide me through the chaos I had created in my life and others. I needed to become alive again and welcome the moments so I could remember that no matter how hard or joyous, with Him I could slay whatever stood in my way.

Oh, and don't you worry about Austin and me. We are grooving so well! Now he is 5'8", plays football, and wrestles. Sometimes

I still see that little boy standing in front of me with his red face and that crazed look in his eyes, stomping his foot and spewing fire! However, now I have the experience, knowledge, and pure will to never stay in the "Quit" when it comes to him! I fight for him to help redirect his storyline and shed light on developing his character's outcome. Why? Because I know that boy will be legendary! Sometimes we need to allow for a wide berth as we enter new sections of life, but at least we have figured out how to co-exist on the same dance floor. We are not always on the same beat or even listening the same song, but when our dances are in sync, no rivals can match us.

You know, it's when you're exhausted with little strength left inside that a dreaded plot twist will emerge and throw you off the path you are meant to journey. They don't seem to shake you quite as much when you're on the true path and plugged into God, when your vision is clear, and you've had eight hours of beauty sleep! But they are patient, like a hunter stalking you, choosing the exact moment to pounce, engulfing you within the darkness in the margins of your story, and casting a net of confusion to ensnare you, while creating division among the characters in your story. It's when you are at your weakest moment that you must decide you will fight. That you will take your "I Quit the Family" moment, journal a new entry, and change the narrative. Some days this is easy, while other days, you must fight over and over again to rally your exhausted, sleeping warrior within.

Luke and I aren't sure how the ending of our story will be remembered, but we are anxiously awaiting for each chapter to unfold. We could share many stories about the struggles with raising our kids, all of the invasive plot twists, or the gathering of our troops when we decided to stand and fight for our own legendary story. From the effects of lifelong medical diagnoses each of our kids will endure to solving the mysteries of relationships from kindergarten to college, to having three mythical creatures known as teenage boys in the house at the same time to that one little princess who, I swear, is ten going on twenty-five, twirls around dancing and daydreaming about her future. We have stories that will make you laugh and, let's face it, at my age almost pee your pants! But what we have learned is that each part of our story we face develops a valuable part of our family's essence. They carve a way through the mountain terrain and the raging rivers of life. They prepare us to keep fighting because we know together that our family is stronger, and we celebrate in the knowing of it. We hope that as we continue living out the yet-to-be-written pages laid before us, no matter what lies ahead, we must keep our focus on the Author of our story and allow Him to develop our characters through challenges, pitfalls, and mysteries filled with twists and turns. Without Him, we would live permanently in the Quit, and we would certainly be missing out on the best parts of our incredible family story! Who wants to miss that?

5
Words You're Not Prepared To Hear

What an incredibly wonderful world we live in. It's full of beautiful flowers, trees, lakes, mountains, and lots of animals for us to enjoy. Each time I stand on the deck outside our home, I am reminded of the natural beauty and incredible sounds God has created. I've even come to love the whimpering sound of our puppy when she wants to come out of her room to play with the kids... well, except when it is 2 a.m. The wind blowing through the trees and the sound of ocean waves falling on the shore are by far some of my favorite sounds in the world! Although I remember not that long ago that some of the sounds I was most hopeful for and looking forward to hearing were our kids' first words. I just knew "Momma" would be the first word out of their mouths! Spoiler alert... it wasn't. Each one of them said "Dada" first. Those stinkers! It's not like I gave birth to them or anything!

As you are becoming a parent, you start to realize there are many things in life you never thought about before and, for that matter, didn't know to even think about. Suddenly, you are thrown into this new, exciting experience of parenthood, and you can become overwhelmed by the numerous questions you have about information you are expected to know! One of the main things you watch for as a new parent is when they reach milestones like talking, crawling, and walking. In general, there is a timeframe for major milestones that doctors watch for to ensure your kid is growing and developing properly. It's important to note that each child is unique and will arrive at these goals at different times, and some kids are considered late in reaching their milestones.

I know that as a new mom, the very first things I noticed were all the sounds coming out of the baby! We are conditioned to pay close attention to sounds they make, especially when they cry. Crying is their only way of communicating to us when something is wrong with them. Parents are on heightened alert when a baby starts screaming. It doesn't even have to be your baby! Any baby will do! It triggers our parenting instincts, but of course we pay super close attention to our own baby's cries. If you've ever had a screaming baby on your hands, you know it's true when I say we will shove practically anything we can find into the baby's mouth, just to stop the screaming! Especially after midnight!

As our kids grow, so do their capabilities to learn and create more sounds. Did you know that babies start to mimic the sounds we make at a very early age? In fact, pediatricians have noted that babies begin to babble at around four months old, and by seven months they have added consonants to their repertoire![1] I don't know why *da* is easier to say than *ma*, but like I said, "Dada" won as the first word for each of my kids. It's incredible to me that our brains can process such intellectual understanding so early without really comprehending much of the world around us.

There are wonderful and funny memories I have with our kids and their first words. I remember their first "I Love You to the Moon and Back," "I Miss You," "Momma, Scratch My Back Please," "Momma, It's Hot as Hell Outside," and the list goes on! He learned about Hell in church and that it's so hot you never want to be there. I guess he was really listening during Sunday school that day and took that story to heart. However, there are some words that wound your heart when you first hear them: words like "I Hate You," "You're the Worst Mom Ever," and others that my kids used in emotional moments trying to lash back at me. We've all heard them as parents, and some of those words sting worse than others.

Sometimes, however, there are words that break through the silence and can never be unspoken. When they land on you, they singe your soul, causing unbelievable anguish and uncertainty. Sometimes, words tell a hard, gut-wrenching truth about your kid, whether it's a medical diagnosis or a secret your child needs to share. I know from experience that you can never be prepared for those moments, and they change the trajectory of your story, leaving you to make sense of the noise caving in around you.

I'll never forget when, at fifteen months old, Cameron was referred to an orthopedic specialist because he wasn't walking properly. My husband was concerned that one ankle seemed a little different than the other, so we decided it was a good idea to see a specialist. Now moms, you know I completed a deep-dive, thousand-hour research study online with quotes outlined from medical journals and books, absorbing all the information I could about his specific symptoms. I was armed and ready to share with the doctor my fully confident diagnosis and treatment plan. In my mind, with his specific symptoms, we were dealing with something called "clubfoot." I was at peace. I had it all planned out; we would obtain the diagnosis, move forward with one of the options for treatment I concluded would be effective, and it would be life as normal. Yeah! Well, that couldn't have been further from reality!

We arrived at the hospital to meet the orthopedic specialist, and as I checked our son in, my husband and both of our moms went to sit in the waiting room. Everyone wanted to be there to support us, no matter the outcome. After a brief wait, a nurse came out to ask us a couple of questions regarding what brought us there. We explained that our son seemed to have a little trouble walking, and his ankle looked different. We assured him it was not very noticeable; he was just having some issues. He asked if our son would walk for him, and I swear to you that when Cameron started walking and limping along like he did, we had never seen anything like it before. He was struggling, dragging his left leg behind him slowly. We looked at each other, eyes wide in complete shock! The look on the nurse's face was what you would call "priceless." His face went sheet-white, and he turned around and practically ran back into the office door from which he had emerged. We busted out laughing! It was the only response we had! We didn't realize it at the time, but that hysterical moment was a blessing for the release of emotions we needed before the doctor's words rang loudly through the air.

When we were finally able to speak with the doctor, he politely listened to each of our concerns and questions, even from each of our moms. He began his examination while we discussed milestones, and he paused occasionally to move Cameron's leg. When he started to move up from his leg to investigate his arm, I thought it was weird, but we went on with the discussion. The more I watched the doctor's exam and his body language change, the more I felt like he was not leaning toward my astute diagnosis!

Once he was satisfied with his physical exam, he wanted to see Cameron run. Not an odd request, really, given the fact that we were there for his ankle. We walked into the hallway, put him down, and turned him loose. When Luke told him to run, his eyes grew big because we never let him run inside buildings. I can still see his little cheeks turning red from excitement as he ran toward me with his blonde hair lifting through the air with each step he took. He looked adorable with his own unique style of running. As I watched him racing toward me, I noticed, as always, how he was skip-running with this leg. But for the first time, my eye caught how his left arm pulled close against his body like a tight hug as he ran. I started to feel a pit form deep within my stomach as Luke and I exchanged glances that shared so much with unspoken words.

As we turned to enter the room, everything started to move in slow motion. My footsteps felt heavy, yet they fell silently on the white tile floor. The door shut heavily behind us, sealing us in without escape as the doctor broke his silence. We were intently listening to his words as they escaped into the air and waited for his thoughts and final diagnosis, but we weren't prepared for his announcement.

"Well, you have the right church, just the wrong pew," he said. As we spared a glance at each other, Luke asked, "What does that mean?" and doctor explained, "Your son has hemiparesis of the left side." To which I said, "Do you mean he is partially paralyzed?" The air was sucked out of the room as sharp inhales from both our moms sitting behind me rang out. And then the doctor spoke those terrifying, life-changing words: "He has Cerebral Palsy." Enter, stage left, both moms sobbing loudly in the background. Luke and I focused on what the doctor explained about the diagnosis, his thoughts for treatment, his prognosis, and our next steps of action for intervention. What we did know was that the earlier he started therapy, the better his muscles would respond.

We were confused as to how this even happened to him, and how we didn't know. The doctor explained that this injury is due to a lack of oxygen to the brain, which can cause damage in vastly different degrees depending on the length of time oxygen was deprived. He also stated that he had seen many young, even teenaged patients, who are brought to him by a concerned parent, only to find out that they have been dealing with CP all that time and had no idea. I remember that Luke asked whether Cameron's CP would worsen, and we were told no. In the big scheme of the actual brain damage, that was true because the damage was already done. However, we had no idea how this would affect his learning ability, walking, or other ongoing capabilities in the future as his body continued to grow.

I wanted answers, tests, and a plan to find out exactly where the injury was located, and how it would impact his future. By the time we left the office that day, we had a plan, a CT scan scheduled, and our moms were consoling each other and us as we were completely drained from what we had just endured. Two words shifted our entire perspective on life. We had more questions than answers, more anger than peace, and I had a deep-seated guilt rising within me. How could this even be real? I had endured so many problems carrying him, especially the pre-term labor and bed rest for months, and my body never progressed to allow his birth. My mind was in a dark place and sinking deeper. After a few weeks passed, during which we had been reflecting on many moments in Cameron's life, one from his delivery came flooding back to me. I knew exactly when his brain damage had occurred. That moment in the operation room, when I was moved to the operating table, and the doctor exclaimed, "Get him out! Get him out now!" Those were the words spoken as Cameron was struggling for oxygen within my body. The sound of those words echoed through my memories, crowding my mind with images of his lifeless body emerging from mine. The cord wrapped twice tightly around his neck, cutting the flow of oxygen to his brain, and his dark blue and purple, limp body being lifted through the air by the doctor handing him to the waiting nurses. Those ninety seconds changed our lives forever, and that frightful cluster of syllables, just seven words vocalized and released into the air, became one of the top three most horrible expressions to touch our lives.

As parents, I believe feeling out of control during an unexpected, adversarial moment is usually our norm. It's that gut reaction, the fight-or-flight response, that overtakes our body. The feeling can grow into a perpetual emotion, however, which creates a never-ending roller coaster ride through life with no emergency exit in sight! How can the sound of small spoken syllables cut a heart so deeply and be so unsettling to the mind that it nearly breaks you to the core? If you're like me, you go through these emotions in about four seconds, and then you start devising a plan of attack! CP and I were going to fight it out, and I started by dusting off and lacing up those red boxing gloves. We dropped a few stools in the corner of the ring because this battle was going until there was a knockout! (And hopefully, it was not going to be me.)

This is where we found ourselves with Cameron's diagnosis, assembling all our courage, energy, resources, and clear mindedness we had to hold our ground and fight. We had to fight because the alternative was to allow this abrupt knowledge to deteriorate the family foundation we had built on faith and hope, and that was not an option. There are many things you will experience along your journey as a parent. Wonderful people will lift you up in prayer, encourage you, or bring you meals. There are those who will take your phone calls in the middle of the night, or better yet, open their door when you show up because you honestly just need someone to hug you and listen to you scream with no judgment. We were so very fortunate to be surrounded by incredible family and friends who prayed over our family with such love.

Unfortunately, no matter how much love surrounds you, moments will arise that try to disjoint your mind, allowing troubling thoughts to materialize. I have been a mom for a long while now, and I am still surprised by comments others make regarding other peoples' children. I have a sweet friend whose daughter is in her early thirties and was diagnosed with CP at a young age. We were sharing our stories recently when she told me that after her daughter was born and she shared the news that she was expecting again, others asked her, "Why would you have more children? Are you not afraid that you will have another child just like her?" So brazen! I am not sure any parent would ever be ready to be asked that question.

I myself was asked an interesting, somewhat similar question years ago, after we became pregnant with our second child. I was with family and friends when a lady asked me, "Are you going to use the same doctors who delivered your first child?" When I affirmed that we were, she said, "Why would you stay with the same doctors after Cameron's birth? How can you even trust them?" I remember answering without giving it much thought, because in my mind it was pretty straightforward. I wouldn't change anything about Cameron. If I did, he wouldn't have his wonderful personality or sweet spirit. God was in control of my delivery scene as it unfolded, and I have no doubts that Cameron is exactly who he is supposed to be. I knew that even through it all, God was in control.

But even knowing that truth, there was still pain in hearing his diagnosis. It was still difficult and downright scary walking through this uncharted journey. Honestly, I was a hot mess most of the time. I had already been struggling with levels of guilt from the delivery. With these additional challenges, I spiraled farther downward, causing me to withdraw even further and create walls around my heart. On occasion, there was reprieve within the chaos. Moments of clarity within. I recall vividly the peace, calm, and purpose that appeared at times. They were fleeting, but when I was blessed with those moments, I clung to them.

Our shocking discoveries along the journey of parenthood did not pause our momentum for long. By the time Ethan was born, we had developed a pretty smooth rhythm with family life. But as I mentioned before, it was stressful juggling therapies, specialists, CP clinical visits, careers, church, and daycare. Ethan was a pretty hilarious kid, but Lord, he was so mean! Around the age of one and a half years old, it was difficult in daycare with him. I remember that he and his playmate Gabriella exchanged bites for months! Every other day, either her mom or I would get notes or even phone calls from the school telling us who bit who first and what the score was for the day. These two definitely had a lot to say to each other, and unfortunately, they decided to communicate through biting! At the height of the exchanges, we had to work out a plan for them to be separated throughout the day and allow only certain times they could play together. Finally, this phase seemed to fade, but it didn't take long for a few other behaviors of his to draw our attention.

During his pre-kindergarten days, signs that he was struggling became more evident. Ethan was running away from the classroom, his teachers, and even the principal. One day, he was brought to the office for misbehaving, but when the door opened, he fled the room! I don't blame him, per se, but this was when he started showing more and more signs of not being able to cope with certain situations. The teachers were concerned about his safety and, of course, so were we. We discussed this with his pediatrician, and we were recommended he see a sensory expert.

Ethan's diagnosis would by far be the longest journey we would walk in this area of our life. From a very young age, we could tell Ethan was smaller than other kids. In fact, when we took him to the pediatrician for his annual checkup and they outlined his growth, he never truly landed on the growth chart. In fact, when he finally broke through that bottom line and landed a solid dot on the curved chart, it was like reaching the top of Mount Everest after being hit by multiple blizzards and freezing temperatures trying to stop you in your tracks! We were ready to throw a party!

For a few years, he continued to grow on his own curve and the doctors didn't seem to be concerned, so neither were we. After all, I am only five feet, two inches tall. It was around the age of ten when he actually dropped off his own chart, and they began to worry, and so did we. It would be years before we would realize why Ethan seemed to not grow as rapidly as other kids.

I remember when we would meet new people, they would ask if Ethan and his younger brother were twins. I hated that question! Especially when Ethan was standing there, because I could see the flash of pain appear in his eyes as he tried to avert them and avoid more attention being brought to him. There were many times during his sports seasons he was unable to participate because he would become sick. He missed more than his fair share of practices and games due to illness. When he was healthy, he did participate in basketball, diving, swimming, and when he joined the water polo team in high school, he found his niche. Each of his coaches would always say, "I wish I could take Ethan's aggressive intensity and put that in my biggest kid on the team!" It was meant as a compliment to his personality, competitive spirit, skill, motivation, and dedication… but came off backhanded by insinuating his body type was wrong. It was hard hearing that feedback over and over again, and it was even more difficult for him.

His actual diagnosis would come the summer before he turned fifteen. We decided to let him go to a dive camp in Georgia with his new team. We were excited for him, but it was nerve-racking for me. He was going to be the only male in a house full of teenage girls and women! The girls were agitated because Ethan being the only boy meant that he got his own room and bathroom, and his very own king size bed! It was pretty hilarious, honestly!

I had checked on Ethan several times during the week, but one evening I received a phone call from one of the "House Moms." These were the moms who went on trips, planned meals, and helped shuttle kids for the coach. When she called, it was a few days before I was supposed to pick him up at the final tournament. This House Mom was a retired nurse, and I knew that her calling meant she was concerned about something going on with him. She informed me that he had not felt well for a few days and was dehydrated from his illness. As she spoke, I could tell that she thought something was really wrong with him. She confirmed my suspicion by telling me I needed to make an appearance in Georgia earlier than expected so that I could see him with my own eyes.

After discussing the situation with Luke, I decided to go down early to spend time with him away from the distractions of our normal life. When I arrived on the scene, he honestly didn't look bad to me. His eyes were dark underneath, but they were practicing a lot, and he wasn't getting a lot of sleep. I asked him how he was doing, and he said he felt better after drinking all the fluids. I really couldn't make out what the big deal was that first day I was with him. The next day, we ate breakfast with the team, hung out and headed for the dive competition. It was an exciting morning watching him and his teammates rally together in support and encourage each other as they jumped off a perfectly fine board! I personally didn't see the appeal!

Finally, after a few hours of waiting, it was Ethan's turn. I remember sitting in the stands on those hard bleacher seats because I had forgotten my nice seat at home. As I was adjusting to make my bottom more comfortable, Ethan was walking towards the diving board, and that's when it happened. He took off his shirt, and I remember staring at him in complete shock. His body looked so frail. I could see each one of his ribs as he breathed and even when he didn't. There were shadows across his side where the skin was sucked in between each rib. I couldn't believe what I was seeing! Is this even the same kid who left me a week ago? I had never seen him look like this! What happened to my baby? I called my husband after I calmed down and tried to maintain some presence of normalcy for Ethan's sake, to share with him that we had a serious problem, and that Ethan was very ill. I didn't know what was wrong, but we were going to find out immediately.

We finished out the day as I tried to hide my growing concern from Ethan, and the next morning we started home. I had already called the doctor on Saturday and made the appointment for first thing Monday morning. They didn't have anything available at first, but I told them they would fit him in because he had to be seen by the pediatrician immediately.

We arrived at the doctor's office Monday and discussed the details of what he experienced on his trip, as well as the previous tests and visits to the main hospital for stomach issues we did the year before, and he examined Ethan as I shared my concerns.

We were relieved, but scared, when we finally received the diagnosis of Crohn's disease. Once again, we heard more words that would affect one of our kids for the rest of his life. The knowing didn't make things easier or more straightforward either. Honestly, even as they painted the picture, shadows seemed to form between the painted strokes creating cracks within the paint. We had yet to comprehend the magnitude of ongoing treatments, tests, procedures, surgeries, and medication trials he would endure for the rest of his life. As the doctors continued to speak, the colors began to blend together and, in some areas, started turning black. His treatment would be like placing pieces in a puzzle together. With the correct pieces, the puzzle picture fits perfectly together. However, if there is a missing piece from the box or a unique piece that just doesn't seem to fit, it can change the entire look or create unfillable holes that need to be fixed.

I believe Luke handled all the stress and chaos better than I did, though it was not really fair to him because I was such an emotional mess, I know he felt that he had to hold it all together. I wish I would have been stronger for him and carried a heavier load in a healthier way, but I just wasn't capable of that yet. I know there were moments he wanted to break down, and there were times he did, but I felt that I failed him during this part of our marriage. It was too much for me to face. Sometimes we would stand holding each other and just cry as we were told yet another prognosis for one of our kids. But in the early onset of our parenting experiences with our first kid, I had begun to withdraw myself, leaving him to pull the edges in like a blanket you fold to swaddle a baby, to hold our family snugly together. It was difficult for us both, and we definitely processed the experiences differently.

We have always been honest with our kids about their diagnoses and let them know that we have their backs. We feel that is the best way to prepare them for their journey ahead and have trust that God will see them through. Cameron once asked me about his CP and why it happened to him. I told him that God created him to be a fighter from the very beginning of his life as evident by his fight to be here with us. He has a special purpose assigned, that only he can accomplish and bring forth. I explained that everyone has something, be it a deep emotional wound or maybe even a scar, they would like to hide from the world. It's just that his "something" happened to be one that others could easily identify. We taught our kids to never be ashamed or try to hide any part of who they are, and we encouraged each of them to fully own who God created them to be, because there was a purpose just waiting to be discovered within. Cameron has a gift that no one else has, and one day, I know he will uncover, embrace, and set it loose in this world.

When Cameron was six, I was pregnant with our third son. I was actually lying on the shower floor with the water on HOT because I was in preterm labor and in so much pain. In the middle of a contraction, he appeared at the bathroom door and asked me, "Mom, do you remember when I went to be with God in Heaven?" In my mind, I was like *What? I can't even right now!* But what I said was, "Yes. Yes, I do." I know he was recalling when he died during birth before God sent him back to us. He had talked about it before. While standing there, he told me "God sent me back because it wasn't time." I about lost it, y'all! I started thinking what is he trying to tell me? Why would he say that, now? I honestly believe he was trying to comfort me while I was laying there in pain, reminding me that God was in control. Cameron has always had a spiritual connection and an insight to wisdom well before he intellectually should be able to comprehend it. I have no doubt that he has been marked by God for more than he can imagine. Each of our kids have this unique piece to them, and sometimes it is the missing connection they forget to grasp during life's troubles. As parents, our role is to help guide them to it and through it and encourage them to be the very best, unique selves they can be.

I must share with you that I always found it amazing that I didn't cry over Cameron's diagnosis. At least not at first. Not even when we shared the news with our extended family. It just never crossed my mind to cry. I was devastated, and sometimes when so many thoughts and emotions hit me at the same time, I either spiral out of control or just go numb. For a long time, numb is where I lived. The way I saw it, we were presented with a challenge, and we were going to manage it head on! I needed a plan to execute so I could move down a checklist to know I was achieving something along the way. I needed something to preoccupy my mind. Do you want to know when I finally cried? It was one evening while rocking him to sleep in his room. His little body was warm, and he was curled up in my lap breathing softly as I patted his back. He was drifting off into sweet dreams, and that's when it hit me! I realized that one day, someone was going to make fun of my baby, call him a name, or even bully him because he was different or because he was wearing a leg brace or because his body didn't work the same as others! That's when the emotions I was holding in broke through, and I sat there sobbing, squeezing him as tight as I could while throwing my hand over my mouth to stifle the anguishing cries that shook my body. You talk about an emotional release!

I don't know how long I sat there holding him, but I remember I was devising plans to make him safe. I rehearsed the words in my mind over and over that I would tell him to say when people asked him what was wrong with his leg or why he walked the way he did. I also may or may have not created several escape plans out of the country just in case Momma had to bring out her full "Chuck Norris" moves on somebody. Just kidding! Maybe. You never really know where your mind will take you when you feel the need to protect your kids, but I knew enough about myself to know I was ready to do whatever it took to do so.

What incredible things will God do with each of my kiddos? I ask myself this question often. I am fortunate that I have a front row seat to the amazing experiences he has waiting for them. I have access to watch them as they grow and learn and build their faith, trusting more in Him; I've already seen how much they have blossomed and how their understanding of what they can achieve has enlarged. Some dreams have come true, and others have morphed into blessings beyond what they could have imagined. Each one of their diagnoses brings something unexpected that touches their lives, but God continues to turn them into new chapters in their story as only He can.

I'm so very strange and, well, human, I guess. Give me something stupid to worry about, and I will whittle time away building a monumental, elaborate kingdom in my mind to fortify myself. But give me a real struggle, one that should bring me to my knees, and I react like a lioness! At least for a while, until my strength runs its course. I found through these times that sustaining the lioness can develop into a crippling numbness that I am unable to escape on my own. My only saving grace was that I had an "exit buddy" riding along with me, and He came with a plan.

There's a Bible verse I clung to through times of trouble and anxiety that has stayed with me to this day:

> For God has not given us a spirit of fear, but of power and of love and of a sound mind.
> *(2 Timothy 1:7)*

These words brought me peace and having traveled through this part of my story, I can promise you they absolutely ring true. This verse was shown to me prior to suffering two miscarriages by my pastor's wife when I told her I felt like I was going to lose a child. She prayed with me and encouraged me to continue to focus on God and His words. I clung to that verse for guidance, for peace, and for seeking my sound mind! We lost our two little babies before we even met them, but I know that I will see them one day, because I have faith in the power of God's Word. His words have carried me through the deep waters of life. I didn't need to worry or judge myself over the past because life is here in this moment! We have the ability to use the power and love God gave us to conquer any fears that try to take root within our life. There are no words that can be breathed over my life unless they pass through God's mighty hands first. I know now that even when I can't find my sound mind, God has me wrapped in His promises. He is there holding all the pieces, catching me when I fall, or putting the pieces back together again. He is always working for my family's good . . . even when I am not prepared to hear those words or face the outcome of their wrath. He is always prepared, and I am never alone.

---

1. Dwyer, Lexi. "When do babies start talking?" TODAY.com. April 11, 2019. https://www.today.com/parents/when-do-babies-start-talking-t149765

6
No! You Can't Touch Me!

God has greatly blessed me indeed as the wife of Luke and the mom of our uniquely amazing kiddos. Raising my kids is one of the most rewarding, joyful happenings in my life. Even in the chaos, and with our differences and strong personalities, somehow, we blossomed through it all. Our journey was cultivated with love, but it was in faith that we continued to walk through adversities together, as we realized hope for what was waiting through our journey.

Being a mom of boys is like riding a motorcycle, running the throttle wide open with no brakes. I knew this life well, being with three boys. I was even prepared for it mostly by my childhood, as I was raised on a street full of boys. However, I knew that when our daughter joined the family, a dynamic shift was going to take place. Even though I had two sisters, I knew nothing about girls or braiding hair. If boys were wild and full of endless energy, girls were full of sassy spice and everything nice! Oh, the days ahead for me would sure be full of stumbling through raising a daughter. I was just hoping I'd make it!

I loved playing games when I was young, especially when I won! Do you remember the games you played as a kid? Games like Kick the Can, Spin the Bottle, and Truth or Dare? What about the "I'm Not Touching You!" game? It's the one where you try to annoy your siblings while sitting in the back seat of the car or in close proximity to them, and you pester them until they scream for you to STOP! I mean, just because you placed your hand ever so closely to their leg doesn't mean you touched them. You may not have been touching, but you were just brushing close enough to their skin they could feel the electric charge pass between you. Yet, you were still "Not Touching" them! Yeah, that's the game, and I hated being on the receiving end of it! I can't even begin to tell you how uncomfortable I feel when someone is in my space. Unless you've been in these situations, you couldn't possibly understand!

I remember a few years ago, I was standing at the Coke machine in a local restaurant to fill my cup with ice and soda. I had just stepped up to place my cup under the spout, when an odd feeling began petitioning my senses for immediate attention. When you are going about your normal day, you are not typically on heightened alert patrolling for danger, and I was in my daily routine, with my guard down. I realized quickly that my body was sending urgent messages to pay attention because the person in line behind me waiting to fill up his cup with ice had breached my comfort zone! Not only did he breach it, the guy was way inside my space. I had to turn and give him a glare which conveyed, "You need to step away from me, and quick!" Finally, I was able to catch his gaze, and he stepped back. I was highly concerned he was going to touch me because I knew I would react in an overly emotional way. Situations such as these triggered for me anxiety, pain, and anger, and my self-defense system would boot up quickly, ready to explode!

The person in line had completely ignored vibes he certainly should have received from me! Not only had he ignored them, but he had also moved closer toward me, inch by inch, pressing his way into my comfort zone! Why? Was he not aware of proper social protocol? Was he unable to sense the weird factor created because he was absolutely too close to another human whom he didn't know?! Or did he know, but just did not care? Maybe he was completely oblivious, but either way, he was definitely way too close for my comfort!

No matter the excuse, his actions created a trigger response for me. As a side note, let me share what I mean by that. In a psychological sense, a trigger is a stimulus such as a smell, sound, sight, or even a word that elicits feelings of trauma. The word itself can be used in many ways. When we are triggered, our minds hurl toward a past trauma, recalling memories, feelings, and stress associated with that pain. It took many years for me to recognize that I was carrying trauma from my childhood experience with the boy at church. Then, I had to discover how that trauma was weaved throughout my life and had manifested itself into my behavior, my relationships, and the decisions I made. Along with that, I had to identify what my triggers were so that when prompted to react, I could learn how to regulate my responses.

After years of reflection on my behaviors, risky decisions, and reactions, I am able to share a few of my main triggers with you. They stem from these common themes of safety, touch, restrictions, manipulation, or the dismissal of my feelings. If I feel that I am being taken advantage of in one of these areas, alarms ring in my mind, and my skin crawls with the stir of anxiety as I fight the urge to erupt in anger. If I experienced the slightest trigger, images would creep into the far edges of my mind, crowding my ability to think clearly and propelling me toward an uncontrollable place! That is, if I am unable to quash it in a timely fashion. The onslaught of emotions can wreak havoc within me as they try to thrust toward the light to expose my vulnerabilities.

The first time you lay eyes on your newborn baby is probably one of the most magical moments a parent will ever experience. Everything about them is wondrous and shrouded in mystery. A feeling of full love and protection rises up within you, out of the blue. You want nothing more than to capture time and slow its pace in order to consume each moment of their life. Time, however, will not lie motionless. It is audacious and requires movement to press forward, even when you are struggling to breathe.

When Brooklynn was born, she was the tiniest, sweetest little thing I'd ever laid eyes on, outside of the times I first laid eyes on my three baby boys. Her head barely filled Luke's hands as he cradled her for her very first photo shoot. She was so cute with her little pink hairbow we glued to her head! I remember her sweet, perfectly pink lips that were formed with a flawless degree of pout, the dark brown birthmark we call a "Kiss from God" on her hand, her dark brown eyes with beautiful green flecks, and her dark brown hair. Her hair was the darkest of all our kids. It only took four tries to get one close to Luke's nearly black hair color! Lord! She was so precious, and with her Daddy's dark coloring, she was a brilliant sight to behold. I won't lie—I was scared to death to be the mom of a little girl! So much so, that when I came home from the hospital, not only did I bring our precious bundle of joy home, but I brought with her a patch of gray hair that had the audacity to expose its menacing self on my head! Right in the front for all to see, too! I call that into evidence as Exhibit A. . . Let the judgment from others begin, y'all!

We brought home our baby girl with gusto! In our minds, if not outwardly! We were three boys and three major medical diagnoses in, and we were truly exhausted! We thought that surely since we had survived this long with each family challenge we faced, we were certainly due a reprieve from emergency room visits, surgeries, and anything that remotely looked like a medical facility! We were so done! Have you been there?

For Luke and me, it never seemed like our parenting experience was straightforward. Even when something started out simple enough, it would become entangled with difficulties crashing and merging together, creating a realm of chaos! It wasn't long after we brought Brooklynn home that she developed breathing issues that sent us to the emergency room repeatedly. We had plenty of experience dealing with this sort of thing, as our boys had spent many days at the hospital with whooping cough, bronchitis, RSV (Respiratory Syncytial Virus), and other respiratory issues. We devoted many nights to lying in bed, watching as one of our kid's chests would rise and fall. It reminded me of watching ocean waves smashing against a beach—If the wave hit too hard, the sandcastles would dissolve quickly, leaving a void on the sand; if it landed too softly, the ocean current slowed, causing risk of not circulating the water properly. But a perfect wave left a clean slate while continuing to move the ocean. Similarly, with our boys, they had to breathe just right and within a certain pattern, to reveal just enough labored breathing to allow for medical treatment.

I remember the agony of watching them struggle to breathe. Many times, I would gently press a finger under their nose checking for signs of life. A gentle touch to their cheek or lips would trigger a nursing reaction, encouraging them to breathe. We would time their breaths per minute and attentively watch for intercostal retractions, which is when the skin is sucked deep between ribs, exposing the delicate framework as air struggled to reach their lungs. We used many tricks and techniques throughout the years with our boys, but there wasn't a trick in our bag to help Brooklynn with the very real diagnosis of Congenital Tracheal Stenosis at the age of eight months. She would struggle to breathe over the years due to a narrowing of her airways. We were so very blessed that time resolved this issue, but there were many sleepless nights of touch and go with our princess along the way.

We knew Brooklynn was the last little baby we would bring home from the hospital, and I wanted to spend as much time with her as possible. Frankly, I worried about her at night because by the time she joined the family, we were so exhausted I wasn't sure we could manage it all! I was pretty concerned we would sleep right through her crying! Luke hadn't woken up in years for the weather sirens in the middle of the night and they weren't that far away. We had less energy and slept much more deeply than we used to. So, to counteract my anxiety, I purchased a little cradle that snuggled directly up to my bed. This way I could get to her immediately once I finally did wake up!

Let me tell you, our little girl was a Daddy's Girl! We would literally joke that Brooklynn didn't even act like I was related to her most of the time, let alone that I gave birth to her. Clearly, the burden of carrying her or taking shots to remain pregnant with her while on bedrest for four months wasn't enough to solidify my status as a priority relationship in her mind! She was clearly her Daddy's baby for the first three years of life. So much to the point that I remember asking Luke one day, "Do you think she will ever at least act like I gave birth to her at some point during her life?"

Well, ask, and you shall receive! You never know what will happen when you ask for something! I will caution you to be very specific about what you ask for, because you may receive it... and then some! When Brooklynn was almost three, we moved from the wonderful house to which we had brought our little babies home from the hospital. We didn't move very far, but we did enter a new school district across the county line. It was the perfect time to transplant, as our oldest son was entering middle school where all elementary schools merged. Basically, no one would be able to identify him as a new student to the school district, thus making it an easier transition for him to make friends.

Two months later, we were moved into our new house. Albeit we were still unpacking boxes and laying out furniture arrangements, but we were in the neighborhood. Not shortly after, Luke needed to travel for work, which rarely happened. It wasn't the best time for us, but it was required. Luke headed down the road for work, and later that night, darkness fell over our new nest while I was busy with the evening routine of getting kids ready for bed. All the usual activities, the normal brushing teeth, taking baths, doing therapies for all the kids, and saying prayers until I was able to finally lie down had taken place that evening with nothing even remotely standing out as notable.

Usually, Brooklynn slept in her own room, but with Luke traveling, I decided to grab a little Momma time with her and let her fall asleep with me. I planned to move her to her bed, but of course I was exhausted and fell asleep beside her! Tell me that hasn't happened to you before? I was asleep soundly, until around 2:30 a.m. when I woke as Brooklynn bolted straight up in bed, gasping for air! I sat up quickly and realized that she couldn't breathe. I could see her little lips turning blue as I whisked up her nightgown to see her ribs fully exposed in intercostal retraction as she tried to move air within. You would think that the first thing I did was call 911, but I didn't! I called my mother-in-law who lives fifteen minutes away. I said, "Lynn she's not breathing! What do I do?" to which she replied, "Call 911—we are on our way!" Now, at this point, I did call 911, and this is where the crazy starts. We had moved to a new area not that far away, but evidently it was far enough to make things complicated.

When they answered the phone, the operator asked me what the emergency was and then where I lived. I explained the situation, and then they asked me which ambulance service they should send? I said, "What? I don't know—just send someone! Send EVERYONE!"

I couldn't believe what I was hearing from the other end of the phone in the midst of Brooklynn's struggle to breathe! I didn't care who they sent as long as someone—*anyone*—with oxygen and the ability to use it arrived quickly! They finally confirmed who they were sending, and I hung up the phone. I know now there are different counties and possibly townships that can run the same routes, so it's a very good idea to confirm who your emergency services groups are, especially when you move. There was nothing to do but wait! Did I mention it was summertime? This is important because it limits my options to treat her. If it were winter, I could take her outside in the cold air. But it was summer, so my only option was to literally take her to the kitchen, open the freezer door, and stick her head in as far as I could! I know this sounds super weird, but I promise this is a real tactic doctors tell you to use and what you have to do when your kid is struggling to breathe with airway restrictions in the summer. The cold air helps! Shortly after, my mother- and father-in-law arrived at the house as the ambulance was in route. We were able to reach the hospital for treatment, and the outcome was joyous! When you're going through these experiences as a mom, your heart waits in agony for the prognosis of any diagnosis your child is given. We continue to be blessed with her health, because as she's grown older, her airway has grown as well and allowed fewer incidents.

This horrible event marked a turning point in our mom-and-daughter relationship as well. It became explicitly clear that Brooklynn had shifted her focus as Daddy's little girl to Momma's right hip! Remember those childhood games I described earlier in the chapter? Well, she and I had an intense game of "Don't Touch ME" going, and I was her intended target, no matter where we were or what was going on. I can confidently share with you that at one point, I felt stalked. I couldn't leave the house without a major scene, and when we would go to a restaurant, she practically had to sit in my lap! Even dropping her off at Grandma's was no fun treat for anyone!

As Brooklynn became older, she gained the keen ability to manipulate my feelings. She could easily make me feel guilty for leaving her to go to work, making her go to school, or giving her any reason to cry. I'm talking about those big, fat crocodile tears, too . . . the ones that drive a dagger through a mom's heart! I couldn't bring myself to let her cry for long periods of time, given her airway issues. However, once she reached the age of six, her airway had grown enough that the episodes minimized. By then, our patterns of interaction were engrained in our lives. Her possessiveness of me did improve over the years; however, our two hardest times during the day continued to be in the morning leaving for school and our bedtime routine.

If Luke woke her up for school, World War III broke loose in the house. She would try to physically escape him by running past, around, or under him to reach me lying in the bed. He would have to make her get ready and take her screaming to the bus stop some mornings. It was beyond awful to listen to the turmoil and her attitude only became worse the older she got. Sometimes I would just lie in bed and cry or laugh because I couldn't cry anymore or bear the scene I knew was taking place. My anxiety was off the charts while suffering through this season!

When I woke her up for school, she would fight me tooth and nail to make it to the bus on time. She started having bellyaches, headaches, toothaches, and anything-in-between-aches to create doubt in my mind that she could be sick so I would break down and let her stay home from school. I explained to her that I wasn't allowed to keep her home unless she had a fever, was vomiting, or had some sign of illness, because school doesn't allow it. You can imagine how much that actually worked! If we didn't make the bus, which was part of her goal because, then I had to drive her to school, where for the better part of third and fourth grade, the teacher, office worker, or therapist had to talk her out of my car or essentially extract her from it! Even when I was able to urge her out and walk her into the school, she would block my exit path by standing in front of me and pushing me back into the school when I tried to leave. The school staff and I became quite familiar with each other, and the nurse suffered with me through every phone call home! She was allowed to call every time she went to the office because I wanted Brooklynn to understand that I was the one telling her she wasn't able to leave school. This made her associate the "No" with me and not the school staff, which I felt was very important. She needed to know that school was safe, everyone was there to help her, and she could talk to them when needed. The nurse and I both celebrated when she stopped calling home after roughly four times a day for three weeks! It was easier for me to tell her no without her standing right in front of me! Anyone else have that problem?

Our bedtime routine was even worse because it disrupted the entire family. This meant she was interfering with her parents' coveted evening time together, as well as my time with the boys to say goodnight prayers and chat about the day. I would put her down to bed, allowing time for sharing about the day, prayers and snuggle time, etc., but she fought me over leaving her room each night. It broke my heart and made me crazy all at the same time! I would cry with sadness, and yet I was angry because I felt she was manipulating my emotions. Remember my triggers? Those would be touch, restrictions, manipulation, or the dismissal of my feelings? She was playing on all of them, down to my last nerve! Luke was upset because I was trying to accommodate her, and he was just over it. He wasn't wrong, but his attitude wasn't super helpful. This continued for the better part of two years before I finally sought out a psychologist to discuss her increasing attachment to me.

Before I took her to speak with a doctor, I already knew her diagnosis. Although hearing it from the mouth of a professional didn't really make me feel better, or validated for that matter. My family has a history of anxiety, so it wasn't surprising when the psychologist confirmed our daughter was suffering with separation anxiety. My cousin suffered horribly from this same diagnosis. His anxiety was so severe as a child that he would hang on to the light pole at the bus stop until his mom could pry his fingers loose and place him on the bus. Once he was on the bus, he was completely fine, but leaving his mom willingly was beyond his capability to process.

That old familiar feeling of guilt and failure started creeping through the cracks against the doors in my mind again, just lying in wait for the opportunity to spring forth to taunt me. This was certainly a health diagnosis that could be passed through genetics, so I was unquestionably partially to blame! For me, conversing with the doctor did at least solidify my suspicion of her diagnosis and the timeframe I believed her separation anxiety appeared. That middle-of-the-night episode when she shot straight up out of bed not breathing? That was it! I became her security blanket, her safe haven, a role she magnified in her mind over time and that skewed how she viewed our relationship.

After all was said and done at the visit, with our situation explained as Brooklynn shared all her thoughts and feelings, the psychologist was ready to reveal an action plan. The psychologist's plan was designed specifically to alter Brooklynn's attachment to me to create a healthier relationship for us to operate within. There were two focused goals: to arrive to the bus on time in the morning without a fight, and to establish a solid bedtime routine with time to say goodnight but establishing a time limit for the additional time I spent with her after the bedtime routine.

When the plan was debuted, I really did almost flip my lid! I'm not even joking when I say that it was a "Thirteen-Step Plan" to keep Brooklynn from crawling back into the womb. When the doctor was halfway through explaining it, my eyes started to glaze over from processing all the details! I know that's horrible to say, but I was more than just a little overwhelmed and confused with it all. It sounded like more work… and that it was going to take months to implement. On the flip side, Brooklynn was super excited and smiling from ear to ear!

Let me introduce you to just a portion of the experience we labored through. Yes, it was a labor with every fiber of my being because Brooklynn was bent on keeping me with her, and I was ending this manipulating, grueling cycle of chaos we'd found ourselves in! Things had to change, or one of us was going to need a lot more therapy... and it wasn't going to be me. Each step was enforced for a week in order to solidify the groundwork and build a successful outcome. Step one was to stick with my current routine, but with a time limit of ten minutes before I was to leave the room. I was doing this, but only loosely enforcing the ten-minute rule and leaving the room when I could sneak away, after she fell asleep, or after I woke up from falling asleep next to her! Okay, I kind of sucked at it! Which is how we ended up with the crazy saga we were living through to begin with. Honestly, I was so exhausted by the end of a day dealing with responsibilities of work, therapies, homework, sports, dogs, etc. that usually I would fall asleep in her bed. Let me tell you, Luke was super happy about that one! Ha . . . Not so much!

The first step lasted for a week, and we did suffer through the overwhelming pain of it as she was not happy when I would try to leave. As we moved into the next few steps, each of which also lasted a week, they went as follows: current routine with five minutes of snuggle only, then five minutes lying next to her with no snuggling, the next routine with five minutes of snuggles and five minutes laying on the opposite side of bed, the next routine with five minutes of snuggles, then sitting on the side of the bed with no touching, and the next routine with five minutes of snuggles, then sitting on the end of the bed with no touching. Do you see how I may have become a little overwhelmed and frustrated with this thirteen-step process presented to me in the office that day?

We were deep into week five conforming to the new plan and honest to God, I thought it was never going to end! This week, of course, was when Brooklynn decided to test my commitment level to the new plan and threaten the very foundation of everything we had established to this point! I was sitting with my back facing her, near the foot of her bed, when it happened. Our bedtime routine was complete, and she was tucked securely under the covers when she gently rolled toward me and whispered in a soft, low voice, "Momma, I know you're not allowed to touch me, but can I touch you?" My very skin began to crawl as I absorbed the significance of her words as they sliced through the air falling on my ears! I felt the scream welling up inside of me and struggled to stifle its escape that would pierce the quiet room.

My head snapped around, and I sternly said, "No! You can't touch me!" as she glared at me with her dark-brown eyes. Thoughts flew through my mind! What was she thinking? We had just finished story time, cuddle time, and followed the plan to a T, and I was not about to allow one action by her, as innocent as it seemed, to undo all the precious ground we had fought so hard to gain!

Within seconds of me saying no, she froze, but it only took moments for movement to ensue. Even in the dark, I could sense her body start to shift. With the small amount of light glowing from the nightlight, I could see the covers rise ever so slightly, as her leg slid slowly towards me. As she crept closer, she curbed the pace and landed within centimeters of touching me! She was so close, I swear I could feel the electricity from her sock reaching through the sheets, giving me the slightest jolt and, covering the distance between us. I jumped up off the bed and said, "I will leave this room if you touch me, and I won't come back!" She could tell by the tone of my voice and my body language that I was perfectly serious! One ray of light landed precisely across her face, and I could see the corners of her mouth turn up into a smile as laughter escaped from her throat! I was beyond annoyed that she thought this was funny! I did sit back down on the bed after a moment, and she sharply rolled over, mainly to give me the cold shoulder. But she did drift off to sleep.

Brooklynn really had a knack for testing all of my coping capabilities! We, or at least I, had been working hard toward a resolution, and I was starting to think that she was satisfied with the way we existed prior to the plan! During the peak of our joined-at-the-hip season, she would scarcely let me out of her sight without a fight. I know that such attention isn't supposed to be a bad thing, but because of the overwhelming demands and their overflow into our evening family routines, it had reached a level of complexity that required intervention! I was determined to reach a breakthrough.

I began to wonder how anyone could handle that level of demand placed on them? Who could deal with being constantly sought after, with someone wanting to touch them constantly? I, for one, was certainly "touched out." I honestly couldn't fathom who that would be, except possibly one person, as I was reminded of stories in the Bible and the descriptions of how people flocked to Jesus. How did He tolerate the constant attention and masses as He traveled? It would have been difficult for Jesus and His disciples to make their way through the streets as the crowds engulfed them. Yet He never ran away or even cringed when someone touched Him! In fact, He often laid hands on those who gathered around Him to speak words over them or to bring healing.

I recalled such a Bible story I learned as a child about a very sick woman found in the Book of Matthew:

> And suddenly, a woman who had a flow of blood for twelve years came from behind and touched the hem of His garment. For she said to herself, "If only I may touch His garment, I shall be made well." But Jesus turned

around, and when He saw her, He said, "Be of good cheer, daughter; your faith has made you well." And the woman was made well from that hour.
(Matthew 9:20-22)

Jesus knew immediately that someone had touched Him, and that power had left Him. Surely, with the crowd pressing intensely against him, there were many who touched Him. Why call out this woman's purposeful touch? Clearly, there was something notable about her. He even asked the disciples, "Who touched me?" Which I'm sure they thought was more than a little funny because everyone was touching Him. I think it's funny, because clearly, He knew who touched Him! So, why ask? I believe that Jesus wanted to provoke her to claim her bold actions, and He wanted to acknowledge publicly that it was by her faith specifically that she was healed! Did you get that? She was determined to reach Him, and she pressed herself into the crowd with an outstretched hand between the people crowding the streets so she could touch just the hem of His robe. Why was she so determined to reach him? What had changed within her? I think she had reached a place inside herself where she fully placed her faith in Him for healing.

This passage has helped guide me through the journey with my sweet daughter and further shed light on our relationship. How are these stories connected? Y'all, this was me! Why was my first action not to reach for Him in faith? Just like her, I wasted so much time focusing on how I could fix my situation. I was lost and felt isolated and disappointed that nothing I tried achieved success! When I was finally desperate, exhausted, and isolated enough, I turned to Him. I had been approaching God for a long time out of desperation instead of taking the opportunity to exercise and strengthen my faith by reaching for Him first! I was relying on my own capabilities with misguided faith in myself, instead of in the One who could change my life. I remained focused on myself for so long that my faith was stagnant, and I only brought it out during times I felt I was facing full destruction. I didn't want to execute faith in God, because placing my faith in Him meant I had to deal with emotions I didn't want to face and confirm my lack of control over my life.

That's where I was living, dependent on myself and others in difficult times and holding back from the very growth that could transform my pain, disappointments, fear, anxiety, and my heart. I'd like to say I learn my lessons the first time, but I'm stubborn. You can ask my parents—it always took me longer than my siblings to learn my lesson! I created an ongoing cycle that became my go-to response and hindered the growth of my Faith in Him. Usually after an experience, I would have the epiphany that I needed to check whether my heart was in touch with Him because of the turmoil. But during it, I was too focused on trying to resolve my problem to reach toward Him for guidance. I'm so thankful God is a patient Father.

You know, God allows difficult moments to reach into our story, to give us the opportunity to grow in faith, set a solid foundation in Him, and reveal His power to us. What about you? Are you reaching for Him during the challenge or as a last resort? Have you learned, as I finally did, to turn to Him first and trust that He will guide you, lead you, and give you strength to fight through the challenges? Have you learned He will never leave you alone?

In the Bible, for those who encountered Jesus, it was about the "act of faith" that brought the possibility of lasting change. From a young age, I have loved the story about the woman touching Jesus's robe and what it represents: faith, bravery, unconditional acceptance, love, and how His power can touch us and create lasting change. As I have experienced more of life's lessons, scripture takes on new meaning and becomes increasingly more personal. I find God in the smallest areas of my life, and I see Him working within the lives of my kids. As a mom, knowing my kids are learning to lean into God first and place their faith in Him is a constant source of joy and comfort.

As parents, we understand how important we are to our kids and how they can teach us wonderful lessons, sometimes at the most embarrassing moments. We can learn directly from them to realize what area of our life needs improvement. Our children have an uncanny way of reflecting our truth back to us when we least expect it, and in the most unusual ways. Just because I am a child of God doesn't mean that my faith can't be misguided or placed on the shelf during overwhelming circumstances. I've always had strong faith, but sometimes I've found that it was untethered from the anchor, sometimes for very long periods. I learned that no matter the circumstances, opening my heart and doing the "hard work" was required to place God at the center of my story.

As I reflected on my relationship with Brooklynn, I realized that she had misplaced her faith in me. I became her security blanket the night of her episode when she woke up unable to breathe and I was physically there for her to cling to. As time passed, the anxiety within her manifested into the fear of separation from me, and she intensified her excuses and behavior to keep me close at all costs. She was trying to protect herself by reaching for me. As her mom, I am one of the main relationships and influences in her life. She learns by watching my example and hearing about my experiences. I don't want to pass on a life lesson of "cling to nothing" responses to any of my kids that could hinder their faith growing in God. I want to share with them a legacy of focusing on Him first with determination and courage required to grow their relationship with Him.

Brooklynn has taught me many lessons over the years, but almost none more important than reminding me I should have been clinging to God, like she was clinging to me. She was determined not to let me go, as if I were giving her breath to live. My goal was never to take away our precious time together and that was her main fear. It was for her to know she's going to be all right, even when I'm out of reach and she's afraid. I wanted her to be confident in knowing God *never* leaves her! In Him she can place her faith continuously. I don't want to miss any moments with my daughter or to shy away from her touch when she is reaching for me. I want her to know I am there for her when she needs me for comfort, security, love, encouragement, and acceptance. But it's also my job to acknowledge that even though I love these moments with her, and they are so very dear to me, she must place her faith in Him. I must encourage her to be determined and to take bold action to create a life of moments lived "in touch" with God.

We were so thankful that our psychologist worked alongside us and incorporated our faith into the treatment plan. I am a firm believer that God can bring miraculous healing to any situation. I also believe that God allows gifted minds to create healing with modern medicine as well. These are very personal decisions we've encountered with the health challenges in our lives, and I am so thankful that God provided an avenue to assist us in our healing, and that we have arrived on the other side of struggles more aware and with stronger faith. Sometimes God answers our prayers for healing with a different path than we expected, whether miraculously or through various forms of treatment. I encourage you to make this very personal decision by being well-informed of the health challenge you are facing and with available treatments, and then prayerfully consider and listen for discernment over the decision you must make.

Today, Brooklynn is out of the woods with her breathing complications. She is a smart, funny, beautiful, quick-witted, super sassy girl who is full of energy! She was created to be more phenomenal than I could've imagined, almost more than I could handle, and absolutely more than I deserved to be blessed with! Believe me when I say she's the perfect little girl for me! We have come a long way, although we still push each other's buttons, and I wouldn't have it any other way. We challenge each other, and we have come to fully embrace our relationship while moving forward with a faith journey rooted in God. I know that even though there are more challenges to face, and our faith will be tested, God will create an everlasting change within our lives along the way. And these moments will bind us together for eternity—through the peace that comes in knowing our stories are merged story lines because of our faith in Him.

Luke and I are so very blessed that each of our kids have a relationship with God. It's through faith that we experience a change within our hearts. That's what you can find, as well, if you will open your heart in faith to Him ...everlasting change. I hope in your lifetime that you give rise to bold action and place your faith in Him so you can stand within the crowd and claim it. In doing so, He will bring everlasting change in your life, and your heart will be "in touch" with Him.

7
I'm Reaching

Do you ever feel like you are reaching out for something that's just outside your grasp?

I've said many times that if I'd had the choice, I would have written a very different story for my family. One where we slept through the nights, our kids were healthy, and certainly without the challenging circumstances we've had to overcome as a family. However, had this been the case, we would have been lulled into a false sense of control, and we wouldn't know the stretching of our faith past our own capabilities; we wouldn't have found ourselves reaching for Him.

In life, you must *go* through some stuff to *get* through some stuff! You most certainly need to have experienced walking in sand to recognize and appreciate solid ground once you reach it. We had hopes and dreams of what we wanted for our life, and some of them came true, some evolved, and some never came to fruition at all. How it all turned out isn't anything like we expected! However, the story continues forward with a turn of each page, and in the end of ours, we do claim victory. We can stand firmly on the lessons acquired because by our faith our victory was sealed. It absolutely didn't occur within the timing we desired or even when we hoped for it; however, it appeared at exactly the essential moment.

When I was growing up, I was never really invited on trips with our extended family members like my older sister and brother were. Somehow, even though I was the most fun kid they had (in my humble opinion), I was always left behind to hang with my parents and, of course, my younger sister once she came along. I never understood why I wasn't invited; however, one day my sister enlightened me with a fascinating story that was so crazy I had to confirm its truth with my parents! She loves to tell the story of why others never wanted to take me with them, and y'all, it's a *beaut*!

My family spent most of our vacations visiting parks or going to my grandparents' farm. So, of course this story starts with a typical family outing to Lookout Mountain in Chattanooga, Tennessee, when I was very young. We loved to visit this area because of the waterfalls, caverns, and trails. My sister was old enough to remember, so she was probably around nine, which would have made me around six. As her story goes, we were headed to the top of the mountain where visitors gathered to see the vast views of the land around the mountain, huge rocks, and the incredible sunrise and sunsets. As we were hiking on the trail through the woods, climbing to reach the famed overlook, I was running ahead of the group. I can't imagine why in the world my parents had me off leash! Literally, I was the poster child for harness-leashing your kids before it was legal! Unfortunately for my dad and mom, I came around just a little before its time!

I want to stop to make sure you understand the location and the terrain of where we were that day. This was a *mountain*! There was a split-rail fence with mesh marking the areas you were allowed to trek and remain safe. But if you were able to make it over that, you could easily fall. This was a seriously dangerous area, and I had not met a fence high enough to contain me. Peering over the edge of the fence looking down, there was nothing but sheer drops to rocks below with some scattered trees covering the side of the mountain all the way down. I don't remember this particular day, but we visited this park enough in my childhood that I remember the area well. You could scan across the horizon for forever, and as your feet reached the flat area at the top of the mountain, loose dirt that was tracked over the rock crunched under your feet. I can't for the life of me figure out why my parents thought it was safe to take ME there! I climbed everything and—surprise, surprise—I was a jumper, too!

We probably were not there long before the craziness began. I was an impulsive kid who tended to get into trouble rather quickly. I just had a knack for leaving panic, stress, and general insanity in my wake! My sister said that she remembers Dad, at one point, turning around and asking, "Where is Andrea?" Well, you can just imagine everyone fanned out scanning the area for me! Then, a few moments later when they could not find me, the gravity of the situation began to unfold before their eyes. They were calling my name as they peered over the edge of the fence, looked down the cliff, and scoured the trail in case I had run ahead. My sister said that while she was looking for me, she heard this little voice saying, "Help! Help!" She followed the voice until she saw me, dangling from a small pine tree down over the edge. Remember, how I loved to climb? Ta-Da!

She ran to get our parents, rushing back with them and pointing to where she found me. She said our dad approached me slowly as not to startle or scare me as he assessed exactly how bad the situation was and figure out how to bring me back up over the edge safely. After thinking for a moment, he calmly said to me, "Andrea, you got yourself out there. Now, you get yourself back." Can you even imagine saying that to your kid as she is dangling from a tree off the edge of a mountain? One slip of my slender fingers, and I could have plummeted to my death! He realized that no matter what he did, he wasn't going to be able to reach me without falling himself. I was just too far away from him. The sheer terror they must have felt, knowing I could fall right there in front of them, and they were completely helpless to my fate. I can visualize my mom on her knees praying that I would survive my current predicament.

My sister didn't include that detail, but knowing my mom, I can totally see it! She taught us to pray.

Over the years, I had acquired a pattern for adventure, and my parents often found me in what they called "creative messes" like this, though none were potentially more perilous than the mountain. Only diving off the back of our boat without a life jacket when I was two years old or climbing the church construction scaffolding to dance on the church rooftop even breached the same category of disaster as my mountain adventure! My dad certainly found me in dangerous situations due to my curious, impulsive behavior, but this one topped them all. I can imagine the scenes of my life flashing before his eyes and him recalling my smile, the sound of my laughter, or the last time he held my tiny hand in his as we walked along, as if he would never experience them again.

In those moments, I'm sure he was aware of his heart racing and beating so fast that it felt as if it would leap from his chest. He could probably feel the lump forming in his throat as he tried to speak without screaming, so that quiet, soothing words would land on my ears. I am positively sure his hands were drenched in sweat, and he was thinking, "Even if I *can* reach her, will she slip right through my hands?" I know without a shadow of a doubt that he was praying—praying that I would be able to scoot close enough for him to reach me, and also praying he wouldn't kill me once I did for scaring him to death!

I'm told that slowly, I crept closer to the rocks, where Dad was waiting with his arms fully outstretched as far as they would go. The pine tree sagged from my body's weight, and each time my small hands reached forward to pull me closer, its needles seemed to dance to a lively tune. There was no solid ground beneath me for my feet to use as a platform to push. I was just there dangling. I never really thought about the roots of a tree, but that tree had to have some deep roots to hold my weight! Deep roots are important and are required to hold a tree in the ground, as well as other things. That day, they helped saved my life. With each movement of my hands, I eventually inched within Dad's reach, and he was able to pull me safely up, back to solid ground!

What a fun day at the park, right? I mean, what parents *wouldn't* want to experience that! I can definitely think of two right away. As I have now heard this story countless times through the years, I have a better appreciation for the story and for why others never took me on vacations with them. I don't blame them at all! I was a complete handful. That is… if you could lay hands on me!

Was that the last thing I jumped off of? Certainly not! Was it the last mountain I would jump adventurously from? Yes! Yes, it was! When things don't go according to plan, what do you do? Do you jump and hang on for dear life and pray that you can find a way through, or do you reach out, hoping God arrives in time? Thank God, I had years of experience climbing trees around my neighborhood when I was young. Even during my childhood, God was preparing and developing my strength so that on that day, I could hold on long enough for my sister to hear my voice, and so my dad could calmly reach out and pull me to safety.

Even though I didn't always recognize them, there were many moments that shaped my life, as well as shaped how I absorbed the world around me. As moms, our focus is to cultivate our kids into the character they are meant to become within their story. Are you viewing them as God views you in your story? Are you using the moments you have experienced up until now to build up, strengthen, grow, and prepare your kids for the challenges still to unfold within the mystery of their story? When you feel as if you are lacking—and we all do—is your first instinct to reach for Him?

Luke and I went walking, running, and crawling (yes, crawling at times!) while navigating through all our challenges. What we expected our life to be together and what it became were two entirely different stories. However, as we continue to move through it, we transform into who we are supposed to be as individuals and as a family. We have seen the other side as well! How, do I know? Because God broke through the Quit that was meant to fragment and tear the pages of our story and used it instead to cultivate growth through renewed faith in Him.

I've learned many things from past experiences, but I know for a fact there are additional lessons within them that I missed. As I press forward on my journey, what draws me back to this moment on the mountain are the fingerprints that God placed all over it and how it is etched across my heart so deeply. My dad truly was a representation of my heavenly Father that day. Each time I went through a crisis, I knew his approach would be calm, because he had a pretty straightforward and logical way of thinking. Even when I could not feel His presence all the time, God was there protecting me, and He continues to reveal that evidence within my ongoing chaotic life. I encounter God in the love He shows my children throughout their uncertain trials and challenges as well. The lessons my kids must learn are not always easy for me to watch, but I know they are essential for them to grow their relationship with God.

Why is it that when we see those we care for most being cared for by God with answered prayers and a path through troubled waters, our faith grows just a little more? Because it's another layer of how God demonstrates His love for us. Each time I see God's work as I walk through life, my faith grows stronger.

Luke and I work together to be God's protectors, teachers—and keepers, really—of our kids. This sets the tone for our children within the family, builds relationships, and lets them know we are always there for them, even in the chaos.

When they reflect on their lives, I hope my kids see how God wanted to be actively written into their life's story, not just an honorable mention in the footnotes. I can't imagine what my life would be like if I had not invited Jesus into my heart all those years ago. In fact, my life without God doesn't work. In my darkest moments, while growing up, within my marriage, becoming a mom, and even when I ran from God, He was patiently waiting for me.

In the serious moments that arise, we are almost paralyzed by knowing we have absolutely no control in the calamity! It is also in these moments that we prove how we genuinely live our life. These are the moments where we become a witness to others, and I have to tell you, I did not always make the best example to share with others! Who do we run to for help? Do we stand firmly, composed as we face the storm, or do we run recklessly toward anything that looks like it will provide a steady calm? I certainly was reckless throughout many of our storms. Is there a part of your story you are neglecting because you are in the Quit? Maybe you are like me, and it's going to take an "I Quit the Family" moment or a mountain to change your perspective. You may even believe that you really are in a place with no way through, under, over, or around it that supports the belief that you can survive this, but I know better than anyone, you can! The best part is that you don't have to do it alone, either. God is right there, waiting, and I wish I could say that it didn't take me long to remember this, but it did. I certainly hope you arrive there much more quickly than I.

I did experience moments of real breakthrough when I was placed directly in the path of seeing God's penmanship blatantly writing the scenes throughout my story, and yet, how quickly I moved on from them was astounding! It happened that way in San Antonio, Texas, during a family vacation. God brought me to my knees in the most frightening moment. We had spent the entire day at a local theme park, enjoying the rides, shows, games, and food. The heat, on the other hand, was immensely oppressive, and Austin, who was two at the time, wasn't feeling well. His belly was upset, and he could barely take any fluids, let alone keep them down. We spent the afternoon caring for him, giving him anything he would drink, staying under sun decks, and placing cool washcloths on his head to keep him from overheating. I should have taken him back to the rental house, but there were thirteen of us stuffed in a passenger van and "Calling an Uber" wasn't really all the rage at that point! He eventually fell asleep and seemed to be doing a little better, but in reality, it was the calm before the storm. We made it home after a completely draining day for Austin and me, and I couldn't wait to lay down in the bed. It was time for showers, prayers, and bed. I grabbed our oldest two boys and took them to their room while Luke was finishing Austin's shower. I was listening to their prayers when I heard Luke scream my name.

This wasn't a normal scream either, y'all. It was the kind of scream that sends shivers down your spine because you know immediately something is horribly wrong! I jumped up from the bed and ran through the door, just missing my sister-in-law in the hallway as she came running too! When I reached them, Luke was practically laying on top of Austin as he was trying to cradle him in his arms while screaming at the same time. I had a difficult time comprehending exactly what was happening, but I saw enough to know that Austin's body was convulsing in a seizure.

I screamed downstairs to my mother-in-law, "Call 911!" Then as I turned back to the bed, Austin's eyes rolled back and Luke screamed, "Stay with me! Stay with me, Austin!" over and over again! At that point, all I knew was that Luke had lost his mind, and I needed to take action! I absolutely couldn't handle the scene playing out in front of me, so I started to prepare for the ambulance ride since clearly, we were headed to the hospital!

I grabbed my purse, his wallet, our shoes, and some clothes for Austin's diaper bag. I was doing all of this while sneaking peeks occasionally at Austin in hopes it was not as horrible as I remembered it to be, but YES, it still was! The 911 operator was giving instructions, but I couldn't hear over Luke's screaming. I finally had to tell him to move back so I could see enough to assess Austin and give accurate details to the operator via my mother-in-law. He was breathing, but his eyes were rolling into the back of his head as his body seized, and we cooled him with warm towels as instructed. Then, right before my eyes, everything changed as foam began to stream from his mouth. It was the worst thing I have ever seen happen to one of my kids, and it brought me to my knees instantly!

That was it! Momma was checked out, and there was no more taking charge and grabbing things for the hospital journey! In that instant, as I fell to my knees all I could do was reach out for God, and I whispered out loud, "Sweet Jesus..." as my hands folded in prayer! That moment, I thought his life was going to end as we were completely helpless, reaching out for a miracle. It seemed like time stood still as I watched him struggle to breathe, his body still jerking and his eyes vacant. I just whispered over and over again, "Sweet Jesus, Sweet Jesus." Luke had become quiet as he stared blankly at Austin. But after a few moments, I noticed less foam escaping his mouth, his body was becoming less rigid, and he started to breathe more normally, albeit not completely normally; but I was going to take what I could get! God was holding Austin in His mighty hands and answering my prayers. I couldn't even form words to express the immediate urgent need and I didn't have to. He knew.

The ambulance arrived, and we were taken to the closest hospital. And later, as we watched him recovering in the hospital bed, the doctors explained that he had experienced a febrile seizure. They stated that because he wasn't feeling well earlier in the day, he probably had an infection which caused a spike in his body temperature, creating the perfect storm for a seizure when Luke gave him a shower to clean him up from the day. The shower caused his body temperature to drop quickly, causing the seizure. We were so thankful our beautiful little guy was going to make a full recovery, and as you can guess, after sleeping in the next morning, life moved on as we settled back into our routines and all the craziness of family life that followed.

You know, perspective is a funny thing. If I am being honest with you, I have to say that every time I had the opportunity to continue to reach out for God after moments like this, it usually just got lost somewhere along in the busyness. It's not that I intentionally did this, of course, as God was always a part of my life, but I had to cloak myself in the chaos so my heart could remain unexposed. I understand now that going through each of my experiences was required for me to arrive exactly where I am today—in a chapter of my life during which I am reaching for Him, and He is invited to be actively involved throughout my story. I had to decide that I wanted Him calling me to claim who I am as He was writing on the pages of my life! I needed my kids to see His words create a story that encouraged and inspired others and for them to learn that He wants to write an amazing story on the pages of their lives. The closer your relationship with Him, the more your kids will realize that *He* is the most relatable part of their stories.

I know how my parents felt in those moments of desperation with me hanging over the side of the cliff. There wasn't a single thing they could do except pray, place their faith in God, and reach out a hand for me. I know there was a level of peace that surrounded them. If there hadn't been, how could my dad have approached me with such steadfast, composed confidence while he was painfully aware of how far I was out of his protective reach! It's almost hauntingly good that God is in complete control of every aspect of our lives. Without us even being aware of His constant presence as we pass through our daily routines, He can create the calm or help us find a fraction of peace in just a moment in order to draw us closer to Him. He can also appear in the perfect storm on a mountain top waiting for someone to reach out for Him.

Maybe your parenting process hasn't led you to one of these vulnerable, gut-wrenching moments in life, and if this is the case, y'all are living my dream! However, for those of us who seem to find ourselves in the Quit, whether we are dangling once again off the cliff or unknowingly living in it, we must keep reaching! Knowing that I am carrying these experiences reminds me that He is lifting me firmly up when I fall and carrying me through when I am burdened and overwhelmed, unable to move.

The biggest thrill of my life is watching the story of each of my kids' lives unfold! God is holding tightly the mystery of their stories, and I see the growth of maturity they gain when facing the words He places across their pages. I hear the words they speak with new knowledge, and I can feel the transformation of their hearts as they place their faith and focus on God.

God's mercy, love, and grace are layered over all the pages of my life. Even when the words fall hard, setting the scene for inkblots, juice stains, scribbled stories, and crayon color pictorials drawn in the margins. He still treasures me enough to write with the details of my life. On our own, we are not able to possess the power required to take our stories to the next level. Only faith in God accomplishes this. God is creating the opportunities and allowing encounters to help us discover our truth and to encourage, guide, and grow us so we gain strength through Him. And we must live out our lives with boldness, so we are able to claim what is required for the next level of our journey! By doing so, we have the chance to understand what faith really means: living a life focused on and reaching for Him, while waiting for the next words to line the pages of our story.

What is your indelible moment that sticks out in your mind? Have you played it over and over again? Or, like me, has this become a story they tell about you? Has this brought you to a crossroads or mountaintop experience yet? I encourage you to write out that story and see what lessons you can find. Not just the obvious points of the story, but where it intersects with how God is with you, protecting and training you for life. Most importantly, what moments can you find when God was revealing Himself to you? We all have obvious moments, but true wisdom is found in the treasures only discovered after peeling back many layers on the observable surface.

For those of you whose indelible moment is laced with pain, I can't stand here on the other side and tell you in truth that the pain will eventually disappear forever, or that memories flee from existence. However, with God leading your heart and focusing your mind, you have a much better chance to heal and to realize peace. By placing your faith in God, you can reach the other side, rise above what this world expects of you, rest on solid ground, and find your true purpose within your story.

The last thing I learned from my mountaintop experience was the power in my jump. Yes, I said it, *jump*! The simple act of leaving the comfort and security of standing on solid ground to jump, however naive or careless that it was—and yes, it was careless, my will to live was greater than my curiosity or carelessness. Kids don't fully understand the risks they place themselves in at times, but when they test the boundaries of safety, they do learn from jumping. Sometimes, the jump is safe, and sometimes it's not; but in living life, the risk is ever present.

As hard as it is to think of myself hanging on to a cliff outside of my dad's reach and how my story could have ended that day, it didn't end there. God had a significant plan for me, and that experience was a building block to set my purpose. What purpose was *in* that jump? A lesson of learning to *reach* and *Who* to reach for.

As long as I know I am walking in God's plan for my life, my purpose continues to rise in my story and my heart can find peace. Don't allow those indelible mountaintop moments or their lessons to become lost in the busyness of life. Those moments can add new unexpected pages to your story, allowing blessings to fill your life. I hope that these moments will bring you humbly before God.

Whatever you do, please never stop reaching for Him!

8
Hallelujah! I Can See the Other Side!

How do you see the other side of your challenge, heartache, or trial when you are living in the chaotic overwhelming mystery of this life? Who do you look to? Well, I'm embarrassed to say that it took me a long time to look in the right direction, at least consistently! Why? Because I thought I was supposed to have it all figured out and I had to handle it all on my own! I was so independent, and I totally blame that elf in *Rudolph the Red-Nosed Reindeer*! I watched that movie every year when I was growing up. Remember, he was thrown out of Santa's workshop because he wanted to be a dentist, and he decided that he could make it on his own. What an inspiration! And when he met Rudolph, then they decided to be independent together!

If I had focused on God, I would have found earlier that He is the calm in the storm, just as my dad was the calm on the mountaintop for me because I was dialed in on his voice and guidance. He gave me a steadfast, assured calm, building my confidence to reach solid ground. While I was focused on reaching safety, God was there with me in the awfulness of what I faced. He was the answer, the power the mercy and the peace. My peace never arrived while I was trying to control my life; I only discovered that by successfully becoming my authentic self and discovering my purpose which, of course, was revealed by God only at the time He designated.

It's the transformation of our hearts during this life that counts. From the time we embark on the journey to the time we reach its pinnacle, there are many peaks and valleys. Right before we reach the top though, that's where the real "danger" of this life awaits! Why is it found here? Because it's when you are at your weakest, most broken, most vulnerable, and you risk living in the Quit, possibly forever.

This is the phase of your story during which you are influenced profoundly by what you continue to carry through life. You have become burdened, past your capability to cope with the certainty of where you find yourself. You could even reject the change required to cast your story in a new light and reach the other side!

But, please let me share with you that *it is in these moments that a life worth living is produced.* We may not see the evidence of a moment's importance while we are living in it, because we are trying to survive, but God wastes nothing. Within every marked-through word, smudged out scene from our memory, or ink drop that touches the page, God can fashion new meaning and generate purpose. His timing is perfect. If we arrive too soon, we miss the intended lesson. If we arrive too late, we miss the opportunity. Reaching the other side is about the journey of your heart finding the peace and the hope contained there. Once you grasp that, there will be echoes of life that you can sense are waiting to penetrate and stir your heart and mind back to familiar places. Those echoes are sometimes filled with tears, pain, screams of frustration, and undeniable waves of emotions traveling as if they were crashing ocean waves threatening to rip away the very peace you found from right under your feet. But focusing on God holds you firmly on solid ground.

Cameron was around the age of seven when he needed some teeth to be pulled. This procedure was going to require anesthesia because he was terrified of needles. He had been in enough hospitals to have acquired that fear all on his own! I spoke in detail with the anesthesiologist prior to the procedure, informing her of his CP and of our concerns as we discussed the plan for the next day. Of course, our plan was thrown to the wind when she was unable to insert the IV line due to his veins rolling around under his arm! About twelve times later, she was finally able to grab a vein, but not before he passed out in the operating chair on the eighth try! He was terrified and exhausted from screaming. I was so mad at the doctor, but in that moment, I had to focus on what Cameron needed. A calm came over me, and I reached for his sweet little face, cradling it between my hands as I spoke calmly through his howls, saying "Cameron, I want you to look at me and focus on my voice. We are going to take deep breaths together, okay." I kept repeating those words to him and telling him that he was very brave, and he would be fine, and just to keep focused on the sound of my voice and breathe.

This calmness did work for a few minutes, and then I recall seeing the whites of his eyes as he desperately tried to peek at his right arm once again to see what was happening! Each time he looked, fear crept further in, and he was back to the chaos. As long as he stayed focused on me, we were in the calm. But as soon as he looked away, started listening to the buzz and beeps of the machines, and focused on the medical team saying things he didn't understand, he lost his peace. Similarly, when we shift our focus from God, fear will try to shatter us and claim our peace. Remaining diligent and clinging to His calm is not only how we survive the storms, but how we grow through them, capture whispers of knowledge, and discover gifts and blessings within. He is waiting for us to move through the valleys to reach the peaks and to claim the peace He holds.

God can break through the Quit that is meant to shatter us and use it to strengthen our faith in him. We have no power to acquire the next level on our own. God is behind this, constantly creating opportunities, allowing opposition during the journey to help us discover our truth, encouraging us, guiding us, and developing us to gain strength through Him. We must live it, but He will give it.

God was able to break through my Quit using a very remarkable tactic! He was able to use the very thing I held so secretively in my heart to topple the walls surrounding it! In the book of Psalms, there is a verse I would like to share with you:

> Surely goodness and mercy shall follow me
> All the days of my life;
> And I will dwell in the house of the Lord
> Forever.
> *(Psalm: 23:6)*

You know, there is something just extraordinary about this verse. It expresses God's love for us and that He is actively seeking after us. It may seem crazy to you that I would still believe this after all that has touched my life and that I can still draw upon the promises God extends in the Bible. Well, I still do. If you will reflect on the word *follow* in the verse, it is beyond perfect. Why? Because it shares that God is pursuing us with intense focus! Focus! I discovered that "follow" has many definitions (thanks to the vastness of Google), and I'll share the two below which I believe embody its ideal meaning in this verse:

1. Be a logical consequence of something.
2. Be concerned with the development of (something)

I love that in the verse, "follow" is used as a logical next step after the words "goodness and mercy." God is seeking after us as a logical consequence of His goodness and mercy! He is concerned with our development and seeking a relationship with us in the details of our lives. For me, knowing this is true is the binding that holds my very story together. It's the truth that enables the words filling the pages of my story to fall into place leading to the other side of every moment.

If you were to ask me when I can best see the other side, I'd tell you that, for real, it's usually around 2:30 a.m., when sleep evades me, and God is actively working on my heart! Understanding His timing is something that escapes me! I am assuming that He believes this time is best because things are quiet, and I am able to focus on the smallest thought or idea fluttering around in my mind. Or maybe, He just thinks it's super funny! Either way, the other side waits for no one. Time flows forward as the words fall across empty pages, propelling your arrival at exactly the right moment, exactly where you are meant to be! Did you think that time ceased moving while waiting for you to arrive? The other side is constantly in motion, while each line drops into your story, and I find that it's how we approach it that matters most. Getting there does require focus (God help me), love, growth, and some sacrifice as well.

If you could change something about your life, would you? Think hard on that, because each outcome you have faced and all the blessings you hold derive from moments of the past. I would only change moments, as long as I ended up in the exact same place I am right now! Therein lies the dilemma. I wouldn't be where I am today, and neither would you. Plus, the Hallelujahs preserved inside that journey would be left unclaimed, and I need all of mine!

Do you ever wake up in the morning and make your kids toast? I'm not sure about your kids, but mine will not eat the burnt edges at all! When they were younger, I would examine each piece and decide which side looked most appealing before slapping some butter, honey, or jam on it and showing it off like my prized apple pie for the county fair! They would squeal with delight as their tastebuds lit up with the assortment of toppings! Unbeknownst to them as they were gobbling it up, I had scraped off any dark or burnt areas they could possibly snub their little noses at, and then covered them in all that sugary sweetness! It certainly made the toast more delicious and helped cover up any unsavory tastes and they were obliviously satisfied. It's just like in life—We are all trying to show our best sides. Some of us are more polished with our approach, but if it's just on the outside, how long will that façade last? If you are unsavory on the inside, there aren't enough sweets in the world to cover it up. I promise you that without change within, there is no chance you will reach the other side.

Once you do arrive there, you may find that there are burnt edges still hanging on. Maybe they're the pain of lost dreams or unforgiveness, or maybe even something that emerges from the footnotes that you thought had been released through the journey. It happens to us all, and I caution you to quickly do the work to let it go. Trust me. I know letting go is difficult, as our burnt edges are familiar and sometimes even comfortable after we get used to them, but once they're released, there is a Hallelujah waiting for you to boldly claim!

Without our experiences and the knowledge acquired, we cannot fully embrace the other side. Through my journey of becoming a mom, I can honestly tell you that I thought I knew a lot of the secretive workings of it all. But just like me, no matter what you think you know or how many books you read to prepare for kiddos, at some point you will experience an "I Quit the Family" moment! There's a verse from the Bible, one I learned a little too late . . . I really wish I would have known this verse prior to having children. I think they left this one out of the version of the Bible I learned!

> "Be strong and of good courage, do not fear nor be afraid of them; for the Lord your God, He is the One who goes with you. He will not leave you nor forsake you."
> *(Deuteronomy 31:6)*

I'm being a little facetious here, but there really were moments in which I was terrified. Not of the kids themselves, but of the potential of an uncontrollable moment that could unhinge our family and make us quit for real!

Do you ever feel God pressing on your heart, but you are unwilling to respond? What are you missing because of your stubbornness? Why are you waiting? Usually, I find that I am preoccupied with my chaos, or I just don't want to hear the message I know He is laying on my heart. It takes me much longer to respond sometimes than I would like to admit, and I know there are so many blessings I missed along the way because of it. He is always seeking us; all we have to do is focus on recognizing His presence in our life.

When I was a young girl, I was playing in my bedroom closet with my sisters when my dad pulled a stunt that I will never forget! We were having the best time playing with our dolls, singing songs and laughing, when all of a sudden, we thought we heard Dad call us. Our ears perked right up a moment later, when we heard him yelling, loud and clear, his words creating a sense of urgency for us to respond. He yelled, "Ice cream! Ice cream!" Well, those closet doors flew open, almost rattling off their hinges as they slammed against the walls! Our baby dolls went flying through the air, left to their own survival as we raced down the hall to be the first one in line to reach him handing out those treats! Much to our disappointment, when we arrived, there was NO ice cream. He explained that he was calling to us for a while trying to get out attention when he realized we either couldn't hear him, we weren't listening, or worse, we heard him but were unwilling to respond. So, he decided to change his approach by changing his words. He thought, "If they can hear me, certainly they will come if I yell 'ice cream'." His tactic worked because yes, we did come running! Though I now realize the lessons hidden within his decision at the time, I sure thought then that it was a pretty dirty, rotten trick to pull.

How do you listen for God? Have you felt like He is calling you, but you are unable to focus on his voice through the echoes or chaos playing in your mind? Or maybe you just act as if you can't hear Him? Better yet, you may answer the call, but you are like, "Hello? God? Can You hold, please?" Not that I have *ever* been guilty of that one . . .

When I am distracted by the ever-growing noise of life, I know my faith is being challenged. I'm going to tell you right now that I don't always appreciate it, either, because often I feel stuck in the crevices and margins of my own narrative. I find it difficult to emerge from the details of everyday life to open my heart to allow work to be done.

I know now that He was guiding me through this stained, tattered, and unpredictable life of mine, even when I couldn't feel his presence. However, the inkblots across my heart were deeply etched, and in those moments, I strived to fill the cracks myself. All the while, God was focused on engraving His love across my heart so that He could write a healing chapter to my story. Can I share a secret with you? God doesn't call the qualified, He qualifies the called. God will never give you more than you can handle, and He will qualify you when called to a purpose. But first you must be willing to listen and respond.

I was in survival mode working through the very real health dangers of my pregnancies and deliveries, educating myself through our children's diagnoses, and attempting to maintain sanity while getting through each day. Many times, it felt as if I were dangling from that tree again, white knuckles clenching branches, with no solid ground beneath my feet, as I slowly made my way back to the mountainside. When you are growing and maturing, your roots are settling in, digging deeper into solid ground. As their network spreads, they are anchoring themselves to hold the weight of their growth, as well as searching for nourishment to survive. Similarly, it is only when you grow and transform within, securing yourself to solid ground, that you are able to one day reach the mountaintop and scream, "Hallelujah! I can finally see the other side!"

Sometimes, it can take years to fully comprehend, and I totally hate to say this, but sometimes the misery you encounter isn't even *for you*! Say what? There are moments in life when God will use your experiences to grow someone else's relationship with Him or open their hearts to Him. Often, those around us see how we operate within the storms to confirm where we place our faith. When God is shining through with the promise of hope because your faith is placed in Him, they experience Him in your story. Our difficult trials test us by exposing our deepest wounds, brokenness, vulnerability, and fears. We must cling to His goodness and mercy in faith, knowing He will never quit on us!

It's hard to view our actions from another's perspective. I believe we see our failures as defeat, when in reality, they are meant to be part of the lessons we should learn. God is waiting for us to discover what is beyond the horizons we can see. He cares when our hearts are breaking in pain, but He also knows what is required for us to encounter the pinnacle of our story at the precise time to unite each storyline in one purpose.

I heard a story once about a man who went out into the ocean, and due to unfortunate circumstances, he was thrown overboard and lost his boat and all survival gear. As he was floating in the water, he was praying, "God please send me help and save me." He had been floating for a while when a man cruised up to him and told him to jump in, that he was there to save him. The man in the water said, "No! I'm waiting for God to save me." The man said, "All right . . . " and left him floating in the water. A bit later, another man come through the area with a boat and offered him a ride to safety. Again, he replied, "No! I'm waiting for God to save me." The man left him floating in the water as his boat pulled away. Well, the man floated in the water until exhaustion overcame him, and he died. When he reached Heaven, God asked him, "What happened?" He replied, "I don't know! I called out asking for help and for You to save me!" God stared back at him and replied, "I sent you two boats! I can't help it that you didn't climb in!"

I've been there, waiting for help to arrive only to realize that it had already appeared! I had just failed to recognize it. Sometimes help shows up in the most unusual ways! It's not enough to simply call out for it. You must listen, open your heart and be willing to receive it. Just like this unfortunate man exhausted from swimming was unable to recognize the help he so desperately needed, if we stay in our challenges and struggle too long without reprieve, we become exhausted and find ourselves unable to listen for, recognize, or respond to help once it arrives.

There were very real moments in my life during which I desperately wanted to skip ahead to a moment of promise because where I was living wasn't sustaining me! I can tell you that in those scenes, some of which flash through my mind even today, I placed my faith in Him, and I was able to hold on to this with certainty. Even through the pain, faith was what comforted my heart because I knew God had more waiting to be revealed! No matter what unfolded, I knew that each part of the story must develop for a new chapter to begin.

I must warn you, and I know some of you already know, but please don't think for one minute that just because you are invited into God's plan for your life, and get a sneak peek, that it's going to arrive smoothly or that you will understand it. You may even end up asking yourself, "Why? Why did I peek behind the curtain and call out for help?" When I found out what part of God's plan was for my life, I found myself lacking in every way and wondering how could I offer anything to a perfect plan He designed. It was only God who could have the clarity, strength, knowledge, and capability to let the words fall across the pages and bind my life in Him. You can have doubts, pain, heartache, joy, tears, frustrations, and self-doubt while still clinging to the promise that God is working for your good! We can scour through the scribbled pages of our lives and, despite the advantage of living it, only God knows the beautiful unfinished story that continues to unfold.

What I do know is that in matters of the heart, it is essential to be honest with yourself. To know what you are willing to sacrifice, labor through, and depart from. Just as life can become an entangled snare, the longer honesty is hidden, the harder it is to emerge from the maze you contrive. Yes, I stumble, fall, and sometimes even create the complicated passages in life that are so taxing to examine, I can only skim the pages. However, I know they were all filtered through the stroke of God's magnificent penmanship.

There is more to life than just waiting for the next best or worst thing to happen. Faith takes action! You can't just sit back and expect that everything will come to you in good measure when it's supposed to. Y'all! This life is worth living! What jumps out at you from the "CliffsNotes" of your life? Would you do anything differently? I absolutely would but it would change the story lines and they could be worse than the ones from my past I secretly loathe.

Life is a crazy ride! From personal experience, I can equate it to riding a horse . . . or a mechanical bull! No need to reread it—you saw what I wrote! In my much younger days, prior to marriage and childbirth, the wonderful sense of excitement just thinking about riding a horse or a mechanical bull made them worth participating in! They were fun, dangerous, and (at least for the latter) definitely not something anyone expected me to do! Most of the time, with horseback riding the experience was pleasant as we trotted down the wooded trails. However, there were few times when my horse and I just didn't seem to be on the same page, and it decided I should get off! Like, right then! I have been thrown from a horse three times. Twice I landed flat on the ground, and the third time, I landed on my feet! It was a good save as, at the time, I was on a hillside and when my cowgirl boots hit the ground, I went sliding! I had a similar experience with the mechanical bull as well! So fun, but I definitely landed flat on more than one occasion. Each time I was thrown off, what do you think happened after I hit the ground? Well, I got right back on! I certainly had no idea what was going to happen, and I didn't care, either. I wasn't about to miss the thrill of the ride!

What do you do when life throws you off? Well, I suppose it depends on how you land. However, there are only a few options whether you land flat or on your feet. You can get up and walk away admitting defeat or (you guessed it) get back on and give it another try! I always try to choose the latter, and believe me, you must make a choice. Even if you choose to do nothing, it is still a choice you made!

Focusing on God through your journey allows you to reconcile that you are living a continuation of experiences through His perfect narrative, and to correct past mistakes, create new beginnings, close difficult chapters, and grow your knowledge and faith. In doing so, you also realize the valuable role you play. Life is happening all around you, so don't just let it happen. In the midst of it all, how you live will shape your mind, heart, and spirit! So, remain vigilant and focused on taking action when God prompts you. Remember, it was always an act of faith in the Bible that opened the possibility for lasting transformation within when someone encountered

Jesus. Recall the woman who reached out just to touch the hem of Jesus's robe for healing? Her act of faith is what brought healing. It is a critical element that allows access to change.

We are privileged to live through and witness the ongoing journey God has planned, not just for ourselves but for our families and those around us who are observing our story. God can use anyone's story to influence, encourage, and guide us in such unbelievable, bewildering ways. He wants to pour out love over the lines of your story and invite you into a relationship with Him.

In those broken moments of my life, I saw a quitter. Well, I sure don't see that quitter anymore! I see a survivor who was being sharpened and honed and prepared to impede the blots spilling onto her pages and onto the pages of her family. I see a warrior who rose through adversity calling out for help and staying alert to listen and act on faith. When I am close to the top of each climb I take, with just a few steps remaining to reach the pinnacle, there are times I can feel that loose dirt shifting beneath my feet again trying to throw me off course. But each time, I become steadier and a little bit faster at the climb. However, as I climb, I am still placing one foot in front of the next, and maybe even needing to grasp handfuls of grass and cling to those tree limbs to complete it; these are the scariest moments, right there when the climb is almost complete, because any misstep can cause a stumble.

Through it all, there was always hope in my heart. Hope is in every new beginning, in the turning of a page, standing on solid ground and declaring "Hallelujah! I can see the other side!" Faith placed securely in Him carries with it the hope of renewal and transformation. In time, another challenge will spring forth with its unforgiving storms and try to reclaim what you have found. But God has prepared a warrior who knows that even when the ground starts to crumble beneath your feet or the peaceful rest you have found is disturbed, He has prepared a way. Each time you will grow stronger and more capable through Him.

Just because you are living in the Quit doesn't mean life stops! There are pages of my story that are almost unrecognizable to me, yet each one was worth living. It's when you have that "I Quit the Family" moment and are at your most desperate that you need to seek God. This is how you change the narrative of your story. When you're in the heat of it, you may start worrying that there are only scraps of paper left for your story. I want you to know that even a scrap of paper is enough for God to create an incredible, masterful story of your life. God pulled my life together with love—one word, and sometimes one letter, at a time. With each capturing a memory, adding gravity, color, shading, or texture. He could illuminate the tiniest detail, to which I may have affixed no merit at the time, which led us down a path of discovering that living in the Quit is still living, and greatness can emerge from it, but you must endure.

I believe that we never become the final version of ourselves, at least not on this side and that's just fine by me! The living is part of our never-ending transformation! Luke and I, well, we aren't sure how the ending of our story will be remembered once the pages are full. I could share many more stories about the struggles we faced and invasive plot twists that threatened to crumble our pages and even light them on fire sometimes from sparks of resentment and unforgiveness harbored along the way, but I would rather reflect on the resilience of our family when we decided to fight for our own legendary story.

Seeing the other side didn't look exactly like what we expected, and I'm so glad. Because it was within all the living, the good and the bad, that the greatest moments of transformation took place in our hearts. Remember what God says in Isaiah 66:9? He will not allow pain without something new being born. *Something new being born*! This should ignite your imagination! Because what God has planned for each of us is so much more wonderful than anything we can dream.

Outside of the painful bit, becoming a mom is a journey you are never ready for. You really can't be prepared for everything you discover along the way. There is excitement and hardship in carrying your little one while they develop inside you. We certainly know there is pain when a baby enters this world! Yet, within that pain there is joy, happiness, sorrow, and so many other emotions we can't explain beholden to that experience. But the season of pain we go through will not last forever. And what we learn through it will help us lean into becoming a mom. It commands life to something within us, and we are never the same because it leaves an untouchable mark upon our hearts.

So, what do you do if you feel that you don't measure up? I want to solve this mystery for you now! First of all, can I just say, "Welcome to the club, y'all!" I've been waiting on you and am super excited you are here! Secondly the secret about this measuring up thing is . . . you never will measure up! Bam! There it is! At least, not according to the worldly expectations we are so obsessed with and focused on.

Through the course of trial and error, I can share that I really don't want to measure up to the world's expectations! Plus, what mom has the time? How did I maneuver around this, you ask? I shifted the focus of my measuring cup and realized that by mixing in a little extra of this and a little less of that, God guided me to the perfect recipe for the authentic me. But here's the thing about me and why my cookies rarely turn out: I don't follow directions! I'm a work in progress like everyone else. It took a long time for me to place my full faith in God, to trust and obey His call for my life. It was only through these actions that I am able to boldly walk in my purpose.

There is a beginning, a middle, and an ending to your story, and it's not over yet! The other side really does exist! I have been there many times, and right now in my life, I find myself there again, resting in the peace. I am just like you—a mom doing the very best she can, praying along the way I don't mess up the kiddos too badly! I understand the storylines touching your life. I know what it's like to have a cold, dark place in your heart filled with hate, fear, humiliation, and many more emotions all at the same time, and what it's like to believe you will never rise above the weight of what is holding you down. I also know that you are a warrior, someone who is yearning to see the other side and is going to boldly claim what God has waiting.

There are many stories I have shared with you, but there are some which must remain unspoken. Some stories remain just between me and God. There is only so much you can share about your life with others. I am sharing with you gently, with love, to encourage you for the long haul. I hope that something within my story guides you to the true hope that is found in a relationship with God. All of us are reaching for something in life. There is something in your heart you are seeking to attain. I was seeking to fix, control, and fill my life with all I thought I required until discovering that truly all I require is found in Him, and it's eternal.

As moms, we are always evolving, forever morphing to meet the unique needs of our family members. This is worth repeating: *I don't think we ever reach our final, fully developed mom stage.* Why not? I think it's because our love is always in motion and seeking to grow for those we care for and deeply love. When you finally reach a place of knowing that the Author of your life is intently focused on every word still drying on the pages of your story, and that He is earnestly seeking a relationship with you, then your hope is constantly renewed. Even if you feel your hope has dried up just like dry bones, God can bring it back to life! It's with this hope that we continue to reach. It's the hope of what's to come in the story still waiting to unfold that continues to draw us in. It holds unknown and unforeseen blessings, possibly the best storylines yet to be written, hidden treasures yet to be exposed just waiting to stir within you the embers that lead to bold action.

I hope you understand and feel in your heart that your story holds meaning, that you are unique, that you are necessary in this exact moment of life you find yourself now, and especially that you are His. Each day I wake up and continue to seek God, thankful for the grace and mercy that touches my life. Some days I do better than others, but I'm thankful He is willing to meet me where I am, and He won't quit on me.

And guess what… He won't quit on you, either! God never "quits the family!"

Conclusion: The Most Important Lesson I Can Share with You

God wants a relationship with you. He is waiting calmly for you to respond. Maybe your biggest fear is of when the words stop falling on the pages of your life. This does not bring me fear, because I know when the words stop in this life, a new story begins.

God is about faith, grace, love, and forgiveness.

> "For God so loved the world that He gave His only begotten Son, that whoever believes in Him should not perish but have everlasting life."
> (John 3:16)

If I didn't know anything else about God, I know from this verse that He loves me. It was through the sacrifice of God's only son that His grace created a way for you to know him.

If you have been encouraged by my story and are curious to learn more, or if would like to share your stories with me, please reach out! I would love the opportunity to share with you and encourage you more.

Lead with love, and as always,

"Be You, 'Cause I'm Taken!"

Acknowledgments

I have to start by thanking my husband, Luke: You continued to focus my mind as this journey unfolded before us. I'm very thankful that our lives were designed to be bound together. God knew I would need someone uniquely capable to stand with me through our journey. I am grateful for your love that keeps the pages of our story turning through the chaos. I appreciate all the grace you have extended through the countless late nights and weekends it took to achieve writing this book. I love you more . . .

My kiddos, Cameron, Ethan, Austin, and Brooklynn: You make each day ring with truth, laughter, and crazy! I can't explain the immense joy it brings me to say that I am your Momma. You each have struggled through this life and emerged on the other side to find peace and hope. As your mom, you have inspired me each day and provided a treasure trove of hilarious moments tucked away within these pages. You constantly encourage me as I watch you place your faith in God during the challenges of your life. I want to thank you for the lessons you have taught me and for still acknowledging that I am your mom!

Mom and Dad, Jim and Elizabeth Brooks: Thank you for all of your encouragement, support, and love through the years. Thank you for teaching me about having a personal relationship with Jesus Christ. It was the most important lesson I ever learned. Even though I didn't always walk a straight line in life, it was by your example that I knew Who to turn to and to place my faith and hope in.

My sister Amber Coyle is mostly to blame for the trouble I found while growing up. Half my trouble was found in trying to protect her and keep her safe from everything I felt was a threat. I started most of my parenting tactics on her, so thanks for the test run, sis! Thank you for always shining light on my truth, even when it is too difficult for me to acknowledge. You continue to motivate me to seek further understanding of life around me and in who God created me to become. Thanks for asking the hard questions that produce change within me and push the boundaries of what I believe I am capable of.

Sonia Jackson Myles: Thank you for calling me back after God woke me up from a perfectly good dream in Las Vegas and told me to call you. I love how God brings people together to show His love for them. I could not have imagined that one phone call would lead me to standing face to face with my purpose that started this journey. Without your gentle, yet firm, push toward calling out God's true purpose for my life, I would still be wondering *What if* . . . You helped me start tearing down the remaining walls that surrounded my heart and allowed me to speak my truths without judgement. Writing my first song was just the beginning of a new chapter in my story. I appreciate your sisterhood, mentorship, friendship, and love.

About the Author

Andrea Holman was raised a Southern girl with roots growing deep within the hills of Tennessee and dreams of her music coming alive on the Nashville scene. Life, however, has a funny way of taking twists and turns along the way, and Andrea found herself in a different sweet spot as a wife and mother living in the heartland of Ohio.

Recently, she decided that there's no better time to pursue one's dreams and live one's best life than in the present. Passion has a way of propelling one forward, and in this new season of dreaming big and living bolder, Andrea has recently released her debut album, *Tent Revival*. She is a singer, songwriter, author, and the host of a nationally syndicated show, *Wake Up Take a Minute!* Through the show she speaks to women across the country, sharing stories about her hilarious and often gut-wrenching experiences as a mom.

Andrea is married to her best friend, Luke Holman. They reside in Cincinnati, Ohio, and are active in the lives of their four children, local community, and church family. To learn more about Andrea, follow her on Facebook or Instagram, and connect with her on LinkedIn or by emailing info@andreaholman.com.

Stay connected with all the latest updates and speaking engagements for

Andrea Holman

Author | Speaker | PodCast Host | Singer

AndreaHolman.com

Catch Andrea on her national weekly Podcast
"WAKE UP AND TAKE A MINUTE"

Available on
iTunes | Google | Spotify | Anchor

Interested in hosting Andrea for your next gathering?

ANDREA HOLMAN is available to speak and sing at your event. She is adaptable to your event needs and is flexible in any setting or venue — whether within large groups, small gatherings, conferences, retreats, hosting and emceeing, plus as a keynote speaker.

For more information visit our website at **AndreaHolman.com**

Contact us directly at **info@AndreaHolman.com**

And make sure to follow us on all our Social platforms

Made in United States
North Haven, CT
21 March 2024

50275274R00114